First published in the United Kingdom in 2019

by MilHouse Publishing

Copyright Suzanne Kelly © 2019

Cover Design by Suzanne Kelly © 2019

ISBN 978-0-9559269-5-2

MilHouse Publishing

Balmedie,

Scotland, AB23 8YH

This is a work of fact. No characters or events are the product of the author's imagination. Any resemblance to real persons living or dead, actual situations or happenings is entirely factual and may be described by the use of opinion and satire. Please do not read if the truth offends you.

Donald Trump

in

Scotland:

The Real Real Deal

How a man with access to obscene amounts of money and yet virtually no taste changed a corner of Scotland. And not for the better.

Suzanne Kelly

Warning: contains satire

Avoid if allergic to facts or truth

Thank you

Sorry for the long list, but I am indebted and grateful. As the odds of my writing another book may be slim, sincere thank you to my supportive family especially Matt, Vic, Nancy and Tom; to friends especially Suzi, Mars, Fleur, Christine, Earl, Vanessa; to everyone at Aberdeen Voice not least Rob, Julie and especially Fred; to Tripping up Trump; to Anthony Baxter and Richard Phinney. To BrewDog, Glenfiddich, and the Deborah Bonham Band -- all of which keep the spirits up. And to absent friends from Aberdeen Voice.

Above all, thank you to the Milne, Munro, Forbes and other families living at Menie who did nothing to deserve Trump.

No one deserves Trump. (Especially not families seeking refuge at America's borders).

"Tomorrow is another day and a future for this country still beckons brightly, we will see it realised even with direct interference and obstruction from those who believe they are in power. The truth has a habit coming to the surface and it will do so, in due course." – David Milne, Menie Estate Resident

7

"From hell's heart I stab at thee!"

> \- Captain Ahab to Moby Dick-- Herman Melville

> \- Captain James T Kirk to Khan

> \- What I (metaphorically) think every time I write about Trump

\#   \#   \#

"Scotland Loves Me" – Donald J Trump, KKK-endorsed 45th President of the United States

"Can I say, on behalf of the Scottish nation, we f***ing don't!" – David Tennant, Scottish actor

\#   \#   \#

"…when you're a star, they let you do it. You can do anything…. Grab 'em by the pussy. You can do anything." – Donald J Trump, whose first wife released a statement alleging he raped her

"If Trump's a sexist I wouldn't be in this job… that's not the man I know" – Sarah Malone: former beauty contestant, 'Face of Aberdeen' Aberdeen Journals Ltd competition winer, Trump Spokesperson, and wife of Damian Bates, former editor for Aberdeen Journals Ltd of the Evening Express and Press & Journal– who is soon to release a book on how wonderful Donald Trump has been for Scotland, with Trump's former Compliance man, George A Sorial.

\#   \#   \#

"In terms of high-end product influx into the US, Russians make up a pretty disproportionate cross-section of a lot of our assets… Say, in Dubai, and certainly with our project in SoHo, and anywhere in New York. We see a lot of money pouring in from Russia" Trump Jr., 2008

"We don't rely on American banks. We have all the funding we need out of Russia." – attributed to Eric Trump c 2014

"We have zero ties to Russian investors" – attributed to Eric Trump c 2017

\#   \#   \#

"I don't mind (criticism) if it's true" – Donald J Trump

"Oh yeah?" – Suzanne Kelly

\#   \#   \#

"The Press and Journal is committed to journalism of the highest standards and we aim to produce our newspaper with accuracy, honesty and fairness." – Aberdeen Journals Ltd website; Damian Bates' former employer

"HA HA HA!" – Much of Scotland

Contents

Introduction

A further book about Donald Trump may seem wholly unnecessary; however, I believe I've come up with a few things that are new. I've set out to create a collection of facts that will put paid to the ensuing book by Sorial and Bates. I also wanted to collect the saga of Trump in Scotland in one compendium, using material from media coverage over the past decade, my own articles, and some new revelations.

Readers of independent online newspaper Aberdeen Voice which I helped contribute to since 2010 may be familiar with some of the material in this book. I am sure its contents will be news to many people, and I am particularly keen to reach these people. Perhaps I won't have nearly as many startling 'reveals' as the forthcoming book by Sorial and Bates undoubtedly must be offering. On 11 June 2019 they release their work 'The Real Deal: My Decade Fighting Battles and Winning Wars with Trump'. Perhaps they'll tell us how smart The Donald is, how he won Scotland over, how lovely the course is and how much better off everyone is since his arrival at Menie.

My book doesn't have anything remotely like that.

I will apologise for switching between first and third person but it seemed at times the best way to put details across was in my own voice. I should apologise too for the extensive use of quotes; however, who said what when is relevant. The quotes selected are not here for padding (I am not trying to write a huge book). Some of these quotes should not be forgotten; some are unbelievable, and quite frankly, they help back up the subjects presented which, when writing about a litigious billionaire, seems prudent. The quotes are from a range of publications and authors, highly respected, established media – the kind Trump hates so much. In using so many quotes I am trying to collect the best writing to support my points, to prove that the material is fact based and researched, and to answer people who still claim things at Menie under Trump are fine and will benefit Scotland. Things are not fine.

For over ten years I've followed Trump's invasion (which seems the apt word) of the Menie Estate, a formerly beautiful, unspoilt coastal corner of North East Aberdeenshire. The peace and environmental character of this area Trump has, in my opinion, shattered. I've watched a resistance movement form, grow, and go UK-wide – arguably global. Anyone who can look at the exploits of Donald and his loss-making course and see it as winning should have gone to Specsavers.

I come from New York, and I shared the strong dislike many New Yorkers have for Trump. I was young, but I was aware of the unbridled ego, the cheap-looking gold veneer on everything from the giant 'TT' letters in the Trump building on 5th through his toilet seats. Maybe Sorial and Bates will write about why a person wants a gold toilet seat or to see his name or initials plastered on as much real estate as possible. Trump's activities in Atlantic City are well known, where gambling and crime caused irreparable damage to lives and the area. Sorial will have been around for some of this; perhaps we will hear about the 'winning' Trump experienced in New Jersey in The Real Deal.

In New York I heard rumblings of illegal immigrants being used as cheap labour; there were whispers of non-white people being deterred from buying Trump properties. Will Sorial cover these issues as 'wars' Trump fought and won?

In the 80s I even did an admittedly amateurish painting based on the sickly bronze-gilt and nauseating pink marble surfaces of Trump Tower; even then Trump seemed to demand some kind of satirical response.

13

I moved to the UK to get away from all the superficial, greedy fakery he represented to me. I eventually moved to Aberdeen – and then Donald came, wanting to build a giant complex where people lived quiet lives in cottages and on working farms, where birds of prey flew overhead, where deer and wildlife thrived beside the sea.

My initial thoughts, shared by some (but alas not by the star-struck people in power) was that he needed a way to escape the tax man and/or that he wanted a quick earner by obtaining planning for hundreds of homes on his newly-purchased Scottish Estate which was largely protected by environmental law.

As to any tax offsets – we may never know as this is the first US president ever not to reveal his tax returns to the public. As to the idea about getting planning permission to make his land vastly increase in value, I think I may be proven right in time - sadly. We should know where the money came from, and Trump's tax records should be made public – as other presidents have done.

What has happened though is that Alex Salmond, then Scottish First Minister, and Scottish Enterprise (an unelected quango with a massive budget and more than a few issues) decided they wanted to help Trump 'win'. Together with a few ambitious local figures, they got Trump his planning permission, lots of puff pieces in the local press, and an honorary degree. Did any of these supporters really believe the obviously-inflated claims – thousands of permanent local jobs, millions flowing into the economy annually? How could they have? 'Didn't they do any research at all?' I wondered.

The Trump organisation was supposed to stick to the approved plan. No points for guessing that he's done as he pleased. For one thing the development has already had some 12

14

retrospective planning approvals which were granted by what to me is an enabling, supine, supportive Aberdeenshire council.

You've Been Trumped and the subsequent two films by Anthony Baxter and Richard Phinney made absolutely clear what was at stake: environment, wildlife, the value of legal protection put on land of special scientific interest, and the quality of life for those people living on the estate who refused to sell to Trump (or to Trump's henchman Neil Hobday who pretended to be a tourist wanting to buy a house in the area offering to buy low). And freedom of the press.

Anyone involved in advancing Trump's planning application is responsible for all that came after it was granted. Anyone who cared to do cursory research would easily have learned how litigious the Trump organisation can be, how many small businesses have been harmed or forced to fold when Trump companies declare bankruptcy, and how some Trump housing/ resort complexes finish up (or more accurately don't finish up). Anyone with access to news would be aware of the thousands of lawsuits Trump has been involved in. No one cared to look at how the purchase was done; I'd raised the issue with the council and law enforcement more than once.

Do we believe Eric Trump when he is reported to have said Russia provided funds, or do we believe Eric Trump when he says Russia provided no funds? Everyone knew Trump was linked to organised crime, something the BBC covered in a Panorama special 'The Trouble With Trump' in July of 2013. And yet, Salmond, Scottish Enterprise, 'experts' such as Professor Bill Ritchie backed the tycoon and the reporters who eventually approved the application. Apparently planning considerations cannot take into account an applicant's past and present bankruptcies, planning disasters, documented use of illegal immigrants, links to organised crime, links to foreign governments. Is it time for planning to get out of its ivory tower? I think so.

Did the 'Trump' name- for reasons I will never understand-
impress Salmond favourably? It certainly seems it did. Are
people really that hungry for money or brushes with famous
people that they'll sell their heritage, laws, environment and
rights down the river? It proved to be the case.

The situation at Menie is a disgrace. No matter what statements
Trump International Golf Links Scotland VP Sarah Malone
Bates issues, no matter how wonderful a picture Bates and
Sorial paint in their new book, planning should have never
been granted. As things stand – not least with questions
hanging over where the money came from to purchase Menie
– Trump should not be allowed to do a single further build on
that land until a full investigation into funding happens, until
meaningful environmental monitoring is imposed, and until
it is agreed there will be no further deviations at all from the
approved plan. My wish is that he would disappear and take
the outline planning for hundreds of houses, hotels, a second
course, and Sarah Malone with him.

It would be better if someone who was a better journalist, a
better satirist, and who was better resourced was in a position
to write this book. Sadly, for better or for worse, my research,
my access to residents, and my articles for Aberdeen Voice
written when I lived in Aberdeen, put me in the frame as the
likely candidate to write this book. If it reads like it was written
on a long commute to and from work over a few months,
there's a reason for that. Since I believe it needs to be written
and needs to come out before whatever Sorial and Bates have
cooked up, then here we are.

Putting out this pre-emptive counterpoint to 'The Real Deal:
My Decade Fighting Battles and Winning Wars with Trump' is
crucially, personally important to me. I genuinely want a wider

circle of people to know what has happened and is happening, with a view to fixing what can be fixed, saving what can be rescued, and for those who are in a position to take some kind of action to do so without any further delay. I want people to see the residents of Menie as the patient, strong, long-suffering innocent victims of this nightmare that they are. Here's to better times ahead – maybe without so much war and so much of what these people call. 'winning.'

Having wracked my brains for nearly five minutes, I came up with over 30 instances of things that seemed a touch more like Trump defeats than Trump wins. Here are some of those instances.

Over to you George and Damian.

Suzanne Kelly

3 June 2019

PS on 14 March Donald J Trump, President of the United States, said in an interview that his supporters could get 'tough'. He said: "I can tell you I have the support of the military, the support of the Bikers for Trump- I have tough people, but they don't play it tough – until they go to a certain point, and then it would be very bad, very bad." The President has just threatened opposition. Aside from a temporary outcry, I don't expect much action. Four journalists were shot dead in Maryland, journalists have been assaulted following Trump's sustained incitements to violence. A letter signed by some 200 journalists, many of whom are retired, read in part: "We denounce Donald Trump's behaviour as unconstitutional, un-American and utterly unlawful and unseemly for the President of the United states and leader of the free world."

Team Trump may have won a few crucial battles – but the wars are not over. It is shameful they got this mammoth scheme approved, but that they got the Grampian Police (now subsumed in Police Scotland) to come up with a human-rights busting special policing policy for Trump – who was then still a private citizen – is hugely worrying and unforgiveable. Thankfully, that experiment has met public outcry.

If for some reason you are still able to support Trump through the sexism, racism, lies and attacks on the environment around the world and support systems for the vulnerable, here's hoping today is the day you change your mind.

Foreword by David Milne

Normally I wouldn't read a book with the foreword written by the publisher, but then I'm not reading this, you are.

Seriously, this is hopefully a temporary filler until we get the final copy from the individual who we want to craft this fine piece of text; but until then we will simply have to do with my rambling efforts.

I first met Suzanne Kelly when she was covering the Trump Story for the Aberdeen Voice and her incredulous approach that such things could happen here, in a supposedly civilised country, made me appreciate that many people did not and would not believe the story, some of those would wilfully deny it, just because they could.

The only people in support of this development appear to be those who personally gain from it, while the rest of the planet loses. This site was unique in Scotland as a mobile dune system, at the time of writing some 40% of that Site of Special Scientific Interest (SSSI) has been destroyed and no longer deserves its designation as a SSSI. This isn't just my opinion it is shared by Scottish Natural Heritage (SNH) who are responsible for such things but somehow still haven't got round to formally publishing their report, even though it has been widely leaked.

This project is seen as laughable locally, the people accept the landscape is gone and cannot be replaced, some still do not know about the suffering of the residents as it was never truly reported locally. Suzanne now tries to inform a wider audience about what happened and is still happening here, she does well. You would do well to read this and appreciate that not everything you read in the mainstream press is true.

My friends and neighbours appreciate the work Suzanne has

done on this project and we all appreciate just how difficult it is to get this information out to a wider audience. Hence the book.

Well done Suzanne, lets see who is listening this time!

I The Players

A book by one of Trump's ex-employees George Sorial with former Aberdeen newspaper editor Damian Bates, 'The Real Deal: My Decade Fighting Battles and Winning Wars with Trump', will be every bit as exciting as it sounds.

Even though Bates and Sorial are famous rich winners, perhaps not everyone is familiar with them or other key personnel in how Trump 'won' Scotland, who are now introduced.

<u>The Authors</u>

George A. Sorial

"More than 95 per cent of the SSSI remains untouched and the ecological diversity of the site remains intact," – George A Sorial

https://www.heraldscotland.com/news/14959284.donald-trumps-two-fingers-to-scotland

"Scottish Natural Heritage has known since August 2016 about the damage to the spectacular sand dune system at Menie Links, inside the protected Foveran Links site, but had been keeping its assessment secret." – Bob Ward, London School of Economics and Political Science http://www.lse.ac.uk/GranthamInstitute/news/trump-golf-course-partially-destroys-site-of-special-scientific-interest/

April 3, 2019: after 12 years of working and winning with Donald J Trump, George A Sorial has just announced he's leaving. If the press is to be believed, he is leaving to concentrate on his forthcoming book. Oddly, some people can't help but wonder if that is the whole truth.

This parting of the ways can only mean a few things: Sorial got fired, he quit (perhaps all that winning was getting to him), or he has realised he possesses a spectacular literary talent, one that his statements for Trump never previously hinted at.

The cover of his forthcoming book has the most breath-taking photo of Donald yet in which he is walking, wearing a suit and that famous wide red tie. Trump's luxurious red locks seem all blonde (or is it grey?) in this striking striding image, and there is nothing at all funny about the proportion of Trump's hands compared to the tent-like suit jacket or the disproportionately-leaner legs sticking out of it like sticks from a marshmallow being toasted. But I digress.

George gets top billing on his book jacket, deservedly so. Ten years fighting battles with Donald Trump and winning! George is billed as 'EVP, The Trump Organization' - which must impress you deeply (not least as he no longer works there): Executive Vice President. If you aren't already excited and poised to buy the hard cover as your finger hovers over the 'purchase' button on Amazon, it gets better: "George Sorial, a top Trump Organization executive, shares behind-the-scenes stories of Trump's leadership, problem solving, and success". It will be fascinating to learn how the inability to remember names, pronounce 'anonymous' or 'origin', and lying incessantly while perpetually munching KFC are no hindrances to success for a white male multi-millionaire. Remember, George is not just another one of the dozens of Executive Vice Presidents but is a top executive. Or he was anyway.

Trump's leadership, problem solving and successes are on display in the White House daily. Clearly none of Mr Sorial's anecdotes will include any actions taken by Donald on the personal business front since the great man ascended to the presidency – this would likely violate the emoluments provisions, and that would never do. Donald seems to choose appointees from his Mar-a-Lago club to key government roles, talk confidential business in front of diners in the clubhouse, appoint Ivanka as some kind of aide, and get Jared security clearance. That was some job George did to ensure all was above board. The country's founding fathers thought people should not profit from a stint in the presidency, and should actually run the nation as if it were somehow a full-time job, not something to do in between cheating at golf. They hadn't anticipated the man with the superior genes and the big brain who golf, skip security briefings and tweet perpetually.

George will be a man with sufficient time to pen a book now that he is no longer chief of compliance. George's excellent stewardship led to a watchdog organisation identifying hundreds of potential conflicts of interest for the POTUS in 2018 alone.

George's boss may be endorsed by the Klu Klux Klan and have occasionally said one or two things others may consider racist. George's boss may mock people as 'snowflakes' for showing sensitivity. But to hear him tell it, George has been the victim of racism too. This came in the form of Councillor Coull of Aberdeenshire – remember the place where they love Trump – writing 'Noo Joysee' in a letter to Sorial. This intolerable act of racism perpetrated against the race of people from Noo Joysee who talk like they are from Noo Joysee was even perpetrated on council notepaper.

The Telegraph covered the story and here's how George reacted to being the victim of 'racism':

"He made fun of my New Jersey accent.

I can respect that he disagrees with what we are doing but when you start making comments which I believe to be racist, I think you have stepped over the line.

I was born in the UK, I have a British passport - I'm as British as he is, and he doesn't have any right to make fun of my accent.

I think the fact that he did it on government paper is an abuse of power. There is never any excuse for a racist attack like that."

That puts America's racial problems into context, doesn't it? Poor Mr Sorial.

We cannot expect the same standards of racism of Trump and Sorial as we can from councillors like Coull. As to being a snowflake, in the face of such blatant provocation, I'm surprised Sorial didn't break down uncontrollably sobbing. Or sue. But remember, if Donald J calls a South American beauty contestant 'Miss Housekeeping,' calls Elizabeth Warren 'Pocahontas' or tweets that Maxine Waters is 'crazy' – that's not racist, it's probably clever or something.

George told the Scotsman newspaper in November 2008 Trump had all the cash needed for the Menie project: "The money is there, ready to be wired at any time. I am not discussing where it is, whether it is in a Scottish bank or what, [I think it's the 'or what' that needs some investigation] but it is earmarked for this project. If we needed to put the development up tomorrow, we have the cash to do that. It is sitting there in the bank and is ready to go."

George's unwillingness to say where the money was coming from did not raise many alarm bells; although Trump was then involved in a court case over the funding of his Chicago Trump International Hotel and Tower. Councillor Paul Johnston of

Aberdeenshire had his doubts, expressing concerns about the project winding up in some half-built limbo -- kind of like it is today -- on the excuse that the offshore windfarms would spoil the view for the wealthy golfers.

It is painful to turn from the subject of George even for a moment, but at least the prospect of essaying forth on the virtues of Damian Bates is consolation.

Damian Bates

"This newspaper has given a voice to all those who have wished to become involved in the debate about Donald Trump's plans. That courtesy was extended to Tripping Up Trump in the belief that it was a bona fide group of local environmentalists. Today, it has been withdrawn." – Press and Journal 12 December 2009

30 August 2017 – a day newspaper crews across the UK mourned: Damian Bates departed Aberdeen Journals Ltd.

As the paper put it in the opening sentence of its homage, "Damian Bates as [sic] stepped down as editor of the Aberdeen Press and Journal after six years.'

It's wonderful when contributions to journalistic integrity get a mention; it's just a pity that no one subbed so much as the first sentence of the fitting tribute.

If you want to know about someone these days, visiting their social media is a great place to start. Damian's Facebook home page, at least in November 2016, demonstrated what a passionate, loving man he is. After viewing picture after picture of his selfies and photos of his beloved car, you might conclude he passionately loves himself and his car.

Damian's Facebook page has gone private more recently, with the exception of his 17 April 2018 photo of what looks like Air Force One. Conspicuous by their absence were any photos of his wife and daughter.

Romeo and Juliet cannot hold a candle to the romantic story of Sarah Malone and Damian Bates. Damian was at the Aberdeen Evening Express, which in a revolutionary form of journalism holds frequent competitions for the most beautiful baby, bride, smile etc. And one such contest was to find- The Face of Aberdeen.

Don't go looking for this competition or its results online, or for photos of the winner Sarah Malone used in the promotions of the time. They seem to have been removed from search engines, possibly under the rather recent 'right to be forgotten' laws. But picture the scene – hard-working newspaper man is going through literally tens of photos of women wanting to be the Face of Aberdeen – and then he sees her. Did he instantly fall in love with the photo? We do know she won the competition, and the two became an item and wed in February 2013. The couple were too modest one supposes to share their happiness with the rest of the world. So, Aberdeen Voice did it for them and broke the story. It is remarkable how both parties avoided any conflict of interest between the small overlap of their respective careers.

What were some of Master Bates big wins at Aberdeen Journals Ltd? Where to start? Fifteen years in the organisation; four at the helm of the Evening Express and then Press and Journal editor since 2011. Damian's commitment to journalistic ethics led to some remarkable investigative reporting. Most of this was at other newspapers. When Aberdeen Voice was campaigning to save a herd of deer from the city council's plans to cull them – to plant trees on a former rubbish tip, the Evening Express reported prominently that 'Two Deer had been found dead ahead of planned cull.' The implication was that the creatures had starved and a cull was a good thing. On investigation, it turned out that two deer had indeed been found dead ahead of the cull: by a full year and of unknown cause. The city knew that it had already wasted nearly £50k on the scheme and a government report spelled out that the soil was not able to support the planned forest: these details didn't trouble the editorship of either title. The council was spending handsomely on advertising with the Bates papers all the while.

There was an occasion when an item appeared in his titles about builder Stewart Milne sending a case of booze as a gift to Aberdeen City planners (which explains quite a lot). Stewart 'two wigs' Milne (he would wear a slightly shorter wig for a bit, then after a few weeks switch to the longer one, telling people unbidden that he'd need a haircut soon) was incandescent. 'One more bad story about me, and I'll pull all my advertising.'

There was no story a local millionaire, billionaire or councillor wanted in the paper that Damian wouldn't thoroughly investigate. He printed favourable articles unflaggingly when billionaire Sir Ian Wood – friend of Trump and former high flyer at Scottish Enterprise -- wanted to take a city centre garden and 'breathe fresh life into the heart of Aberdeen.'

For months which seemed like decades to city residents, article after article told us how taking land given to the people of Aberdeen and handing it to a limited company (stocked with associates of Wood's) was the way forward. Photos of Wood superimposed on artists renditions of 'The Granite Web' park design seemed to appear in most issues of the Evening Express and the Press & Journal. The subject of Sir Ian Wood will be covered shortly.

Before leaving the topic of Union Terrace Gardens, there was one instance when the P&J (or as some call it the P & Poo) printed on its cover a box with 'ten facts' as to what the Granite Web (as Wood's plan was called) would provide. This ran from more jobs to influxes of tourists keen to run up and down ramps in Aberdeen in winter, etc. The facts were not actually facts but projections, and a complaint was submitted to the Press Complaints Commission (member of an editorial committee of the PCC – one D Bates). Eventually the august editors concluded that if someone took the time to read the entire boring article, spread over several pages, they would have realised the box labelled facts were not really facts at all. So, that was all right by them, and they decided there was no intention to mislead the public.

Damian was made a 'visiting professor of Journalism' at RGU where he passes his high moral code of journalistic ethics on to others. RGU is linked to Sir Ian, where as Chancellor Sir Ian Wood has a multi-million-pound building named after him. (More on Wood shortly). The building is great; RGU employees have been culled and many are less than happy with their remuneration.

Aberdeen Voice acquired a letter which a complaining P&J reader wrote to Bates and this reply:

"You make some rather pointed but unsubstantiated claims that the paper has personal and political relationships that cloud its coverage. I'm not sure who or what you are alluding to but nothing could be further from the truth.

… when it comes to producing a balanced report in the news pages, we always give both sides of the argument unless that opportunity to respond is rejected. [of course they do – it was just a coincidence that Damian announced that the anti-Trump group Tripping up Trump was in his eyes not a 'bona fide'

28

group]

If you would like to suggest who we are politically-colluding with, I'd be happy to reassure you that it's not the case – what I do love is the fact that I get criticism in equal measure from all parts of the political spectrum and that we open up our columns to people of all political hues to give their opinions. That's what any good journalist should do: No fear, nor favour. [Does Damian still want suggestions as to whom any collusion might have been with? There are a few that come to mind]

Again, I'm not sure what personal relationships you are alluding to [surely not being Mr Trump spokesman clandestinely while editing the papers] but I can guarantee that we never, ever produce content on the basis of a relationship. There have been some rather petty and hilariously wide-of-the-mark allegations made against us for our support of other projects in the region by people who don't like them.

Some people who call themselves journalists are nothing of the sort; they throw mud without any evidence as it suits their particular ideology and then claim others are biased! [Fancy that! Who can he mean?]

If you would like to give me examples of the kind of sinister conspiracy you think we are perpetuating and I will seek to reassure you that we are not."

Master Bates wrote these lines in May 2016, while married to Trump Spokeswoman, just for the record.

The story first broke in Aberdeen Voice; Private Eye (the UK's best source for news and humour) wrote shortly after:

"As reported in Eye 1334, the Aberdeen Press & Journal newspaper has been cheering on bewigged megalomaniac Donald Trump in his bid to turn Scotland into an enormous golf course. The paper's glowing coverage of Trump's resort may or may not be related to the fact that editor Damian Bates is married to Trump's chief spin doctor Sarah Malone."

Despite Bate's coyness over his marriage, his conveniently flexible moral code, and his announcement he would not run press releases or news about Tripping Up Trump (so much for the balanced news coverage he boasted of in his letter), Damian will have applied all of his journalistic integrity, honesty, and sense of fair play to the book he has co-authored, soon to be available to adoring readers, many of whom are hoping the work will include lots of photos of Damian and his cars.

Sarah Malone Bates

The Spokesperson, The VP, The Editor's Wife, The Beauty Contestant and The Councillor's Daughter

"The creation of Trump International has been a gamechanger for the leisure and tourism sector in the region and Scotland as a whole. There are many more phases to come, which will play a major part in the economic future of Aberdeen and Aberdeenshire." - Sarah Malone Bates, Face of Aberdeen, https://www.dailyrecord.co.uk/news/Scottish-news/make-america-great-again-campaigners-7547658

"By his own admission, Mr Trump has created no more than 200 of his promised 6,000 jobs and is thought to have spent just £25m on the scheme while bulldozing environmentally sensitive areas of the Scottish coast" – The Independent https://www.independent.co.uk/news/uk/home-news/Donald-trump-fails-to-deliver-on-golf-resorts-jobs-pledge-8693854.html

Sarah Malone is wife to Master Bates, VP and spokesperson to Donald J Trump and now his son at the Menie Estate, Face of Aberdeen, and daughter to former Aberdeenshire Councillor Tom Malone. How lucky can one gal get?

If you look at the organisational charts of multinational, multimillion-pound, real estate development firms, I bet you won't find too many women in top jobs. Well, at least not very many who aren't architects, planners, engineer or top MBA grads. You'll probably not find many who have made the leap from beauty contestant and museum worker to Vice President and spokesperson. Sarah has broken the mould. It seems Trump is a believer in women in top jobs, whatever level of qualifications they lack. Where better to learn how to manage a multi-million-dollar, international, controversial construction, design and engineering project than as vice president of a project given special government clearance that is meant to adhere strictly to the approved plan?

Sarah seems to have told the Herald in an early interview she had degrees from Glasgow and Cambridge. Brains and beauty? She was, alas, forced to clarify her statement by admitting she had actually done a course in Glasgow and had a degree from a polytechnic in Cambridge, which is not quite the same thing as holding an Oxbridge degree. If you're wondering why you didn't see her on University Challenge, this could be why.

The Gordon Highlanders Museum is a pleasant enough place; it runs dinners for up to 20 people, has a fine collection of memorabilia, and undertook renovations Sarah claimed to have been in charge of. It has not, however, taken over a site with SSSI protections, built a golf course and planned a second one, applied to create 900 homes, a hotel, residential space for on-site workers and a golf club with a restaurant. Going out on a limb, the move from the museum to Menie is just a little bit of a stretch promotion wise, however many beauty contest tiaras you have. Some people think that beauty competitions are an anachronism that belongs in the distant past. How else will Trump recruit his execs, and how else can he arrange to walk in on changing rooms full of young women?

31

As a spokesperson Sarah's not put a foot wrong on social media. That is because she has no public-facing accounts for her role. Emails requesting quotes for publication go unanswered more often than not (although Sorial replied to the AV); and the last time Sarah was face to face with a small contingent from Aberdeen Voice at a public meeting about the possible second course, she shouted at the group that she 'knew we didn't want the second golf course built!'. No, there is no fooling Sarah Malone Bates.

Perhaps a small but telling anecdote involves a press photographer wanting to take Malone-Bates' photo on the Trump course; she was reputedly reticent to leave her office and go into the cold and wind (note to planners – the world's rich are not exactly dying to play golf year-round in an isolated, freezing, windy part of Scotland or buy houses there). However, the photographer persuaded her by telling her how the light was just perfect for her complexion and how lovely she'd look. Out she went.

She's not been hindered by having Tom Malone, former Aberdeenshire councillor, as a father. Whether or not he ever declared his family's interest in Menie and how he voted on wind farm applications lie buried in the annals of Aberdeenshire Council's files and web pages. The council was asked to provide the voting record, and helpfully returned a large list of documents for the author to go through. I'll do that once I conqueor the Augean Stables. How precisely Bates and Sorial will address Trump's failure to halt the offshore turbines which clearly irk him to vexation will interesting to see. At the time of writing, the Scottish government seems to be trying to get Trump to pay for the legal costs. They'd better not be holding their breath.

Alex Salmond

First Minister of Scotland and MSP for East Aberdeenshire
'I'll have the lobster' – what Alex may have said when
dining with Trump, October 2007

Salmond was Scotland's First Minister, and arguably should
have ensured that legal protection given to parts of Menie was
more important than building yet another golf course. He had
a responsibility to ensure that the highest legal protection given
to land, the Site of Special Scientific Interest designation, was
upheld. He had a duty to his constituents in Menie: he never
visited them.

It should be noted that a delegation of Labour councillors
including the late Labour MP Frank Doran visited the residents,
held long talks, and were trying to help. Did either Salmond
or his underling do anything to reschedule? No Salmond visit
ever happened.

Back to Salmond. Sharing wine, steak and lobster, he well
and truly seemed in a bromance with Donald J Trump. That
is all rather straightforward. Things then get a bit complex,
ultimately spelling out how impartiality and non-interference
in the Scottish government of Salmond were flexible
considerations.

The first planning application came before Aberdeenshire
Council's infrastructure services committee and it was
defeated by Martin Ford's deciding vote in November 2006.
Unsurprisingly the papers under Damian Bates' stewardship
blasted Ford and the other councillors who opposed Trump.
Unsurprisingly, Bates said nothing about his relationship with
Malone. What should have happened next was that the Trump
organisation regrouped and submitted a revised proposal.

Instead, Salmond swept in, and took the planning process out of local hands and made it a national matter.

A lot was wrong with what happened next – an awful lot. Some issues will be looked at elsewhere in this book; a fuller report can be found online at http://menie-estate-report.yolasite. com/.

Did Salmond keep trying to help his friend Trump? It seems so. Could things get uglier? Absolutely. Or as Duncan MacNeil put it so well:

"On Thursday 29 November 2007, Aberdeenshire Council's infrastructure services committee refused consent for the Trump Organization's planned development at Menie estate. On Monday 3 December, the First Minister met representatives of the Trump Organization, at their request. At 2.20 pm on Tuesday 4 December, the chief planner met representatives of the Trump Organization, at their request. At 3.45 on the same day, the chief planner phoned the Cabinet Secretary for Finance and Sustainable Growth recommending that the application be called in; the cabinet secretary agreed. At 5 pm on the same day, the application was called in. Cynics might say that Trump said, "Jump!" and the First Minister of Scotland asked, "How high?""

Could things get even uglier still? After the friendship was as dead as the withered grass on the Trump Menie greens after a sandstorm, Trump wrote bizarre letters to Salmond; Salmond published these rants. Salmond called Trump a loser when the windfarm finally got the go ahead despite Trump's machinations. As a reminder, Trump is due to pay the legal costs for the court actions; we'll see what happens with that. On it goes. Salmond calls Trump a 'complete nincompoop'; Trump's spokesperson (Sarah?) calls Salmond a has-been. But the damage is done to the land and the people, people Salmond even now can't or won't face who deserve at least a personal apology. Everyone who wasn't 'Blinded by the Bling,' to use the title of the David Milne (my chosen publisher) book, saw Trump as a man not to get into bed with.

Salmond is currently accused of sexual assault and rape. As indeed Mr Trump has been accused on a number of occasions including the odd statement from Ivana – which is only to be published in full according to the odd legal disclaimer accompanying it. Perhaps we need more discernment in future in choosing who our elected representatives and our celebrities are going to be? Perhaps a country's government should also consider the reputation of the people it aligns with over its own citizens?

Tom Malone

Councillor, Daddy, Father-in-Law

"No gifts, no hospitality, one non-financial interests [church elder]" - Register of Members' interests, -- Notice of registrable interests report for Tom Malone, father of Sarah Malone, Trump Menie spokeswoman; father-in-law of Damian Bates, Aberdeen Journals Ltd editor c 2014.

With Sarah Malone's father an Aberdeenshire councillor; her beau in charge of the only local printed press, Sarah must have seemed a great candidate to head the Trump development, experience notwithstanding and non-existent. Who's the daddy?

Malone of Peterhead was elected in 2012 and stepped down in January 2017 on the grounds of ill health. His register of interest forms with the council that Aberdeen Voice has been able to see so far record no gifts or hospitality received, no shares, no business interests and one declared interest in the Peterhead Common Good Fund. He is an elder of Foundation

Church, and sat on the Buchan Area Committee. He once reported:

"I am leader of a youth music project called 'Blues Tunes' based in Peterhead. I work as a volunteer and receive no financial remunerations".

These interests all sound rather dry if not sweet; whether he should have recorded somewhere that his daughter worked for DJ Trump is apparently not something that he or the council found worthy of noting, well known as it must have been.

Where there's a church and a Trump connection, can some charming evangelical preachers be far away? Indeed not. Mr Malone is an evangelist, and in his own words he 'got saved age 23' and is 'Co-founder and joint leader of Foundation Fellowship of Peterhead. For the divine Will Graham, grandson of evangelist US preacher Billy Graham graced northeast Scotland with a visit in September of 2016. Where would you have learnt of this epic tour if you lived in the area? From the Press and Journal, which wrote.

"The preacher confirmed he was aware many people in Aberdeenshire were suffering from the collapse in the price of oil.

And he responded: 'I would say that the current realities in Aberdeenshire and North East Scotland will help to inform my visit and my messages.

'I say that because when people are hurting, when the economy is struggling and people realise, they don't have all the answers, then they are looking for hope.'"

A US preacher, linked to Trump, used the P&J to say oil prices were collapsing and the economy was struggling (has he seen American poverty I wonder?) ... almost as if to point to salvation coming in the form of Trump and the millions he would bring in. The bellicose kumquat brought instead lawsuits, damaged environment, stalled offshore wind turbine jobs and huge expense to taxpayers in police costs and the cost of his legal action against the windfarm, but there you go.

The word was that Graham would be visiting Trump's premises, if not staying there for some of his time (as befits someone who presumably takes the Bible's fable about rich men getting into heaven as easy as fitting through the eye of a needle). The P&J piece makes no reference to the visit, but handily tagged the piece with 'Billy Graham,' 'Will Graham' and (capitals are theirs) 'TRUMP INTERNATIONAL GOLF LINKS SCOTLAND.' If anyone were confused as to where this economic salvation god's own messenger was promising would come from, they needed only cast their eyes a little further down the internet page to find TIGLS was the implied saviour. Praise the Lord.

Sadly, the author did not manage to get a ticket to any of the Graham rallies. In the USA the evangelicals are pulling the stops out to support god's representative on earth, Donald J Trump. Atwood's 'The Handmaid's Tale' is looking more like their blueprint than a warning: some states such as Ohio, Alabama and Missouria are considering a life sentence or death penalty to anyone involved in abortion (which throws a new light on the evangelist commitment to the 'right to life'). Donald himself famously told an interviewer during his presidential campaign that 'women should be punished' if abortion were illegal and they had one. Bet that got the religious far right voters ecstatic. Looking at what is happening to women's access to healthcare and the right to choose an abortion in US states like Georgia, it looks as if the pseudo-Christian, fundamentalist, evangelical preachers have a foothold.

Franklin Graham, head of the Billy Graham Evangelistic Association chose scripture for the Trump inauguration. White House press secretary Sarah Sanders thinks some god or other chose Trump; close Trump cabal members Mike Pence, Ben Carson and Mike Huckabee are all evangelicals. Jim Bakker: God Chose Trump so Christians Could Prepare For the End Times, and funnily enough some of the white supremacist would-be terrorists who support Trump subscribe to this nonsense. From insane bomber to TV church preacher, there are no shortage of people convinced Drumpf is here to save us.

God help us all.

David Ewen

The penultimate Press & Journal Trump hagiographer

"No one could have foreseen the extraordinary saga that would unfold - one that started with an argument about sand and led to an attempt to bring down a government; that raised profound questions about our relationship with the planet and the power of celebrity; and that forced a reticent people to fight for their own dreams." – synopsis on Amazon for David Ewen's 'Chasing Paradise' book on Trump

If you haven't enjoyed my prose so far (which is understandable), or my lack of deference to Trump (which is less so), you might be better suited to a book written by Trump enthusiast and former Press & Journal man, David Ewen.

"Chasing Paradise" came out in September 2010; it can still be found on Amazon with the cover's grinning bouffant-haired Trump (teeth a perfect wall of white) with a photo of Farmer Michael Forbes, arms crossed and looking (understandably cross).

The Amazon blurb may or may not have been written by the P&J hack, but it does set the tone of the tome pretty well:

"Golfers spend their lives chasing the perfect shot. Donald Trump chased the perfect course. The American tycoon scoured the planet for a site. When he settled on a secluded but dramatic corner of Scotland - his ancestral home and the place the game originated - it seemed like a 'tap in'. No one could have foreseen the extraordinary saga that would unfold - one that started with an argument about sand [well, that puts paid to an entire ecosystem and the value of Scottish SSSI legal protection – it's just sand] and led to an attempt to bring down a government [did it??]; that raised profound questions about our relationship with the planet and the power of celebrity; and that forced a reticent people to fight for their own dreams. This is the story of the world's most charismatic billionaire [sick] and his quest to create paradise."

NB printing the above in full is not an attempt at padding out this book; editing a single syllable seemed wrong.

Did Amazon's reviewers agree with this assessment – that 'the world's most charismatic billionaire' scoured the planet on a quest to create paradise? Not so much.

The reviews range from ever so slightly negative to one love letter.

Love: "I have just finished reading the book and found it to be very entertaining, well written and surprisingly objective, especially when considering that it is Donald Trump himself that forwards the book" – 'Mr Tee'

Ouch: "This book (if I can even call it that), has to be one of the most poorly written, dullest, boring books I have ever wasted my time on. If you want facts and information about Donald Trump's golf course, you're not going to find it in this waste of paper." – 'Sea near Egyptian'

Very ouch: "FFS. What a ridiculous lot of tosh. It's not even built yet. Trump is not a purveyor of dreams, but is destroying paradise. Hideous, hideous hideous." - Jenny

If you hurry, the book is still available on Amazon.

David E doesn't just write about Trump. He covered Sarah's appointment to TIGLS in 2009 in the usual glowing terms. Can you guess what newspaper his article appeared in? I think you can. Ewen wrote:

"UNTIL now she has worked behind the scenes, breathing life into a North-east museum and turning it into a top attraction. [what is it with P&J hacks and the 'breathing new life' phrase?

Is it in their contract they have to use it?]

Now all eyes will be on Sarah Malone herself – as head of Donald Trump's £1 billion golf resort near Balmedie.

She vowed to play her part in delivering a project that would "floodlight" the North-east. [well, it certainly has attracted attention; you have to give Ewen that]

We have a world-class developer whose brand is associated with luxury and excellence' [and sexism, racism, and habitual lying].

Today, Donald Trump junior welcomed her to the team.

He said: 'We were impressed with her distinguished career and the fact she was well-respected in Aberdeenshire was important.

She will be involved in all aspects of management and will complement our talented team'."

Sir Ian Wood

Last but not least, the man behind the curtain:

"[this honorary degree is given] in recognition of your visionary, world-class golf investment which, in spite of a vocal minority, is widely welcomed by the people of the north-east of Scotland". – RGU Chancellor, Sir Ian Wood to Donald. [A 'minority' of over 80,000 people demanded and secured the degree's removal] -

https://www.independent.co.uk/news/uk/this-britain-teed-off-the-residents-of-foveran-links-speak-out-about-donald-trump-s-golf-project-7939044.html

Trump is so burdened by the swell job he's doing as president that he can't spell his wife's name right, calls Tim Cook 'Tim Apple' (and Cook brilliantly changed his Twitter handle to reflect the moniker), and says 'Donald J Trump' in speeches more than he says anything else (except when calling Mexicans drug dealers and rapists, suggesting protestors/journalists be roughed up, etc). You would think there were better candidates to receive a university doctorate. But everyone needs friends of a similar ilk, and Tump's good friend in Scotland is Sir Ian Wood.

Sir Ian is a very smart man. He is very clever at things like offshore payroll machinations that manage to shelter money from tax. Some say his Aberdeen oil industry concern The Wood Groups offshore payroll scheme avoided tax to the tune of £15 million per year. This is fine though, as occasionally he donates money for parking lots and charities.

Despite being a billionaire, his Wood Family Trust billed Aberdeen City Council some £20k a few years back. This was for a scheme that had school children choose charities and make them battle it out for a donation in an all or nothing scenario: very educational indeed, if neither are particularly kindly nor charitable. The city meanwhile is gearing up for another round of cuts, but the billionaire got his £20k from the taxpayer.

His charitable foundations have seen millions streaming in and out over the years, and in 2016 had expenses of about £46 million, based on data held by the Scottish Charity Register. In 2012 it was sitting on some £30 million. It seemed to be paying rather handsome pensions to Wood family Trust members. Parties to these various changing trusts include a Jennifer Craw. Ms Craw has been promoted with Wood's help to head Scottish Enterprise Grampian and hold posts at Robert Gordon University, where a Wood Building was recently constructed for tens of millions. Craw however is a story for another book. Wood deserves an encyclopaedia.

Here is where Donald comes in. Robert Gordon University decided (perhaps with some encouragement from Sir Ian) to give Donald J Trump an honorary degree. The photos of Sir Ian and Donald in their robes (thank god they weren't unrobed) holding the honorary degree are something special. Don't look for a reprint in the Bates/Sorial offering however.

On the day faculty, staff and students were kept well away from the two billionaires by security guards. From all accounts, no one was unhappy about this move. Whether visiting professor Damian Bates attended the grand occasion is unknown, and we can only speculate how inspirational the sight of Wood and Trump in gowns shaking hands must have been for students.

A petition was started to revoke the degree by the writer; it swiftly grew to over 80,000 signatures. Signatories wrote of their rejection of prejudice and hate speech; but it's likely they were just jealous of Trump's good looks, brains and athleticism.

There were students who somehow felt that Trump did not reflect their values and their ideas about inclusion.

The petition read:

"We respectfully request that Robert Gordon University (Aberdeen) strips Donald Trump of the honorary degree it bestowed on him with immediate effect.

"We feel that Donald Trump's unrepentant, persistent verbal attacks on various groups of people based on nationality, religion, race and physical abilities are a huge detriment to RGU. Hate speech must not have a place in academia, in politics or on the world stage. We are confident RGU will agree with the petitioners, and act swiftly.

"We would also note the brave opposition of Dr David Kennedy to [returning] this degree at the time it was bestowed."

Dr Kennedy, long associated with academia in Aberdeenshire and with RGU, had returned his own honorary degree to RGU, somehow not wanting to be associated with Trump.

It is said that the decision to take away the degree did not go down splendidly well at Trump HQ.

The head of the university was in effect forced to rescind the diploma in December 2015; Sir Ian, usually known for being easy going and not at all being a control freak, was said to be slightly unhappy at his gesture to Trump going awry. A few years passed, and the RGU head who had made the call found himself ousted over an RGU deal involving a friend without apparently making the details of the relationship clear. One assumes the relationship between Wood and Craw has been made abundantly clear to any RGU scrutineers and is fully above board – whatever anyone else might unkindly think.

Wood's and Salmond's letters back and forth seem rather

friendly and familiar; some of these letters were revealed as part of FOI requests.

Mr Sorial made good use of Jennifer. Footage of her and the SE Grampian logo were used in a presentation to the council at a town hall meeting. Pity he hadn't asked for permission to use the footage, which anyone might have assumed signalled official support for the project (see Appendix II).

Wood is remembered in the city's outsider artist community for a remark reportedly made on two separate occasions to two different arts practitioners. "Nothing goes on in this town without my say-so" the billionaire said according to Aberdeen Voice sources. If Sir Ian cares to comment, the book will be updated with either his confirmation or denial.

Supporting cast

There are many more players who helped bring Trump's 'paradise' to Menie, not least Jack McConnell, the former First Minister, Scottish Enterprise exec, who said:

"Donald has shown me a real passion for Scotland. He is a globally recognised figure who can help us to promote Scotland. I am delighted that he has taken up my offer [precisely what McConnell offered The Donald should be investigated further]. This is a good bit of business for all concerned."

Others include Perry from Scottish Enterprise, apoplectic police officers who arrested journalists, discouraging police officers who talked photographers out of pressing charges against security guards, planning officers, professors and councillors. For now, their stories will have to wait.

But they are not forgotten.

I. How the Scots were won (or not)

Fighting Battles. Winning Wars. Real Estate Development sounds like a testing ground for toxic manhood in the Sorial/Bates book blurb. Multi-million-pound deals, international locations – wars to be won and battles to be fought. Captain Bone Spurs never saw any real battles; Donald J Trump had a letter from a doctor, giving him exemption from the US draft on account of his osteo-ails aka bone spurs: which are normally curable by the way. His heroism on the college basketball court is the stuff of legend, painful though those bone spurs must have been. Still, our brave soldier Donald fought on, like a real winner does.

Side of Trump's parking lot – plastic blowing into environment (we tried to pick some up). Trump is known for (wrongly) calling out his neighbours for their housekeeping (S Kelly)

What winning could mean to Sorial

Does Sorial count among his battlefield victories the numerous and occasionally frivolous lawsuits, incomplete developments, unhappy home purchasers, the Trump University scandal, bankruptcies which crushed small companies but left Trump unscathed? Do the 'wins' include Trump deals in the Middle East disintegrating (due in some small part to his Muslim US travel ban), the Trump name coming off buildings in Canada and elsewhere, not to mention the unravelling threads of Manafort, Cohen, etc? Does threatening to take 80-something year-old Molly Forbes to court get the Sorial fist-pump of victory? Is having a loss-posting, half-completed property in Scotland where many locals passionately detest the Trump brand get counted as a win? So. Much. Winning.

Granted, the Trump team successfully made Alex Salmond fall for the Menie plan. Alex prematurely called it in for central government handling, and from there the planning permission seemed and was certain. But then came the plans for offshore wind farms near The Donald. He and Sorial fought. They lost. They appealed. They lost again. They angered many people looking for cleaner energy and jobs in the process.

The wind farms are now spinning away across the waters from the Trump property, much to Agent Orange's ire. Despite all Trumps legal wrangling, perhaps getting the planning permission for his golf complex was a rather Pyrrhic victory if a victory at all. If Trump truly believed that wind turbines' noises cause cancer (yes, he did claim as much), and their unsightliness would put off his fellow golfers, then Trump's lost. On the other hand, if he was only truly interested in getting permission for hundreds of houses – which was hardly likely to be granted to any Scottish developer – then it is a win. For now.

The most audacious 'win' for team Trump may be how in the world they convinced a once-respected doctor to say that DJT is a 6'3", 185 lb man in great health. Before Sorial gets his writs out, I challenge Donald Trump to get his height and weight done in front of UK press, with me doing my height and weight simultaneously. I am 5'9 ½" and 180 pounds (I could be slimmer, but I'm much too fond of BrewDog and chocolate, and rarely find enough time to exercise). If it is proven Donald weighs only five more pounds than I do, and yet is 5 ½" taller than I am by an independent team of UK doctors, then I will agree to never write another word on Trump again.

Everyone is tired of Trump's talk of winning and winners, losing and losers. It's bad enough to see everything in terms of black and white, but to not be able to discern your failures from your victories is more than a little worrying in a man with nuclear codes who wanted to throw himself a yuge military parade.

Trump defeats large and small in Scotland must have been humiliating for such an egotistical, insecure ego. How the catalogue of failures can be dressed as a series of battles won will be a masterclass in the art of writing.

What winning seems to mean to Master Bates

If a person's social media pages are anything to go by, Mr Bates wants fast, shiny powerful sports cars, sun glasses, and to be seen with the rich and infamous, viz his photo in front of Air Force One and The White House (more on that shortly). Let's hope his proximity to presidential power doesn't provoke any widening of any of the many investigations into Trump taking place in different parts of America. After all, Trump is not supposed to be mixing US Presidential affairs with private business interests, even if it is to get out a book.

Some might wonder how a man outed as promoting his wife's business interests in newspapers he controlled while refusing to see the opposition as bona fide can walk around without feeling humiliation and mortification. You have to hand it to Bates; his skin is thick.

Now about all this winning: let's see who's won and who's lost what battles.

II. Scottish Skirmishes

These are the losses large and small as they happened at Menie and elsewhere in the UK. Some may be ongoing struggles; some are small wins and some are battles that got international attention. Here is how Trump fared in combat against the Menie residents, the Scots and the UK as a whole, in no particular order:

1: Salmondgate – Alex bent the rules: standoff

One minute it's 2006, and you're flying on the private Trump jet eating Trump steak and drinking Trump wine. The next minute you're taking a plan out of local government's control to the central government, and surprisingly, things go the way of your pal with the private Trump jet. Then you're accused of meddling with the procedures and get your wrists slapped. Then the bromance ends as suddenly as it began with you saying your former friend has a character problem (understatement of the year award goes to AS), while he calls you an embarrassment to Scotland. It's an unpredictable life as Scotland's First Minister.

At the time of writing Alex Salmond has some very serious

charges hanging over him of sexual assault. It's for the law to decide the truth of the matter. What is clear is that when he was in power, he bent the rules to suit his new friend as already shown.

In doing so, he was following a pattern set by the extremely obliging Jack McConnell, former First Minister. In 2006 McConnell, as reported in the Scotsman, broke the ministerial code. As the Scotsman put it in their April 2006 piece:

"… on planning issues, the ministerial code of conduct clearly stipulates that ministers "must do nothing which might be seen as prejudicial to that process, particularly in advance of the decision being taken".

"It adds: "Action that might be viewed as being prejudicial includes meeting the developer or objectors to discuss the proposal, but not meeting all parties with an interest in the decision.""

Jack was happy to break the rules, as was Alex later on. According to the article:

"Hobday said: "Jack McConnell has done a fantastic job fighting for Scotland the Brand.

"He got on the plane to New York and shook Donald Trump's hand. That the First Minister of Scotland went to see him and said we would love to have your resort in Scotland made a big impression."

Hobday said that as far as the Trump organisation was concerned, the resort was a "done deal".

As they say in Private Eye Magazine, 'So That's all right then.'

Back to Alex. As First Minister he should have been a neutral figure in the proceedings. He later claimed, when confronted with how he miserably failed to be neutral, said he was representing his constituents at Menie – you know, the ones who he had never visited at the estate because he was too busy hanging with The Donald. Some might call that duplicitous; it is clearly in violation of the ministerial code of conduct.

The Telegraph covered the slightly complex saga very well, with lashings of good quotes. In their piece of 14 December 2007 "Salmond faces sleaze claims in Trump row' they set the sleaze out nicely. Highlights from their article include:

"Aberdeenshire council officials disclosed that they had to terminate a telephone discussion with Jim McKinnon, Scotland's chief planner, on the disputed application, when they realised that members of the Trump Organisation were in his office."

"The phone call was just hours before Mr McKinnon informed councillors that Scottish ministers had taken control of the planning decision, and less than a day after Mr Salmond met with Mr Trump's team."

"It also emerged that John Swinney, Scotland's Finance Minister, who will make the final decision on the scheme, had visited Mr Trump's New York country club two days earlier. Officials insist he was there on business and did not meet any representative of Mr Trump."

"Mr Trump's application ...was turned down by Aberdeenshire council's planning committee on a casting vote on Thursday, Nov 29. Three days later... Mr Swinney attended an event at the Westchester country club, in New York, owned by Mr Trump. Officials insist that the minister had no discussions with any representative of Trump while he was there."

A cynic might ask 'How plausible is it Swinney didn't see a single Trump representative while at the Trump property at the same time the First Minister was bromancing Trump while a massive Trump project was being called in?'

The article continues:

"Nicol Stephen, the Scottish Lib Dem Leader, told Mr Salmond that his administration "smells of sleaze" over the scandal." Every step of the way there is contradiction, concealment and cleverness from his government on this issue," he added."

"The next day Mr Salmond met with Neil Hobday, project manager of the proposed resort, and George Sorial, Mr Trump's right-hand man, at the Marcliffe hotel in Aberdeen."

As an aside, followers of the Trump at Menie saga may remember Hobday's role in trying to pave the way on the ground. He posed as a tourist, and went to the door of several residents and tried to buy their property. He represented to the Milnes, Munros and Forbes families that he and his wife had fallen in love with the area while on holiday. Hobday said he wanted to buy a home to live in – for far less money than the homes would be worth if Trump got his planning permission. He tried this ploy using an assumed name. Funnily enough, the Munros, Milnes and Forbes chose not to sell up. Funnily enough, this attempt by a Trump project manager to cheat his constituents wasn't sufficient reason for Alex to go and visit them. If you want to talk in terms of winning and losing – this was a disastrous public relations loss for the bald orange windbag. Note to would-be agents of subterfuge: When you need to make up a pseudonym, don't use your middle names – it could just get back to you - right Neil?

When the Shire council turned the plan down, Trump's people then threatened to pull out of Scotland (if only!) and said they would not follow the traditional route of just re-submitting revised plans to the local council.

Back to the Telegraph's account:

"On the afternoon of Tuesday, Dec 4, Mr McKinnon rang Alan Campbell, chief executive of Aberdeenshire council. During their conversation Mr Campbell became aware that two of Mr Trump's representatives, again Mr Hobday and Mr Sorial, were in the room. He asked that the men leave before the conversation resumed. Just hours later Mr McKinnon rang back to inform the council that the application was being called in by Scottish ministers."

And the Telegraph coup de grace:

"That evening journalists were told that the First Minister had had no contact with any representatives of Mr Trump in the run up to that decision. However, it emerged last weekend that Mr Salmond had held the meeting at the Marcliffe".

The Marcliffe is the homophobic Stewart Spence's hotel where Trump often stayed, where Spence dubbed the term 'The Trump Factor' for all the increase in tourism his small hotel (which he tried to sell) was having (a claim successfully challenged by Aberdeen Voice). (Spence had to apologise after making homophobic remarks in a speech – to a body concerned with encouraging tourism).

Law, ethics planning rules, environmental protection were ignored for Trump as previously demonstrated. The people who have helped foist him on Scotland have on occasion been discovered lying, breaking ministerial codes, bending laws, overruling or ignoring planning laws and agreed plans, arresting or threatening journalists, breaching human rights. They seem to do so with complete impunity – and some do it with relish, viz the angry policeman immortalised in 'You've Been Trumped' putting the cuffs on Anthony Baxter. There should have been a proper Holyrood enquiry into all these issues as David Milne's petition sought: it was a ridiculous, intelligence-insulting whitewash which will be covered later.

You might think that a lawyer like Sorial would find his name appearing in such accounts an appalling reputational hit. Apparently, you would be wrong. Surely a lawyer has some clue about propriety, and a lawyer wanting to do business in a foreign country might want to look at their laws and customs. Sorial seems to have been untroubled by the ministerial code of conduct; was it a case of wanting to 'win' at any cost, a belief Trump can do anything he wants anywhere in the world, ignorance of international law, or something else? Only George can answer that one. However, if it were ignorance of Scottish law, that could go some way to the anger and shock that the Trump camp seem to have over the Scottish right to roam laws, which mean people can access the estate and cross the golf course any time they want for leisure reasons. They really don't seem to like this at all. Please go visit if you can.

There is some consolation in the fact so much of this sleaze went public, the relationship soured badly, and that people who actually care about laws, people and environmental protection were fully clued up to what Trump meant, and outside of the Press & Journal or Evening Express, pretending Trump was a great saviour for Scotland was no longer possible. Still, some people will do anything to be close to the rich and famous – however those riches or fame were acquired.

Those constituents Salmond said he was representing? He stood them up as previously described. Alex Salmond did not visit the estate, talk face to face with the people he'd sold out. He never stood on Leyton Farm Road to see the bunds and the dying trees, to meet a woman in her 80s who had to carry water from a stream. He bottled it.

Whatever Salmond has subsequently cried about Trump misleading him or letting Scotland down is hogwash, issued after the horse had bolted: Salmond is no idiot and knew what Trump projects were like and what his reputation was. The buck stops with him.

The buck however first started its journey of being passed around with McConnell, who should not be forgotten.

2. The battle of Glenfiddich – does my arse look petty in this?: loss

There is admittedly a small thrill to be had when The Donald gets angry over people defying him. However petty a matter may seem to you, to me, or to any rational adult, Drumpf is ready to lose his stuff at the drop of a hat. It's wonderful, and making him throw a childish temper tantrum is a weapon that should be used against him more often.

The beautiful, Trump- free haven that is whisky country in the wild borders of Aberdeenshire and MacDuff, The Cabrach, is where you'll find the beautiful Glenfiddich Distillery. The Grant Gordon family are among the wealthiest people in Scotland – and are very kind and down-to-earth with it. They also seem to care a great deal about the welfare of others and the environment. A visit to their family seat would leave a guest impressed by history and warmth unlike the ostentatious displays of marble veneer, cheap gold plating and designer labels that Trump residences are known for. The distillery is spotless and delightful in its countryside setting, with an art gallery, restaurant and shop. Trump and Melania would probably hate it.

The family must have been surprised at the venom Trump directed their way when the public voted for Michael Forbes to be their Glenfiddich Top Scot of the Year in 2012. What was a simple award in celebration of a Scottish spirit and a means to honour someone wound up with Trump making one of his sweeping decrees:-

"Glenfiddich should be ashamed of themselves for granting this award to Forbes, just for the sake of publicity.

"Glenfiddich is upset that we created our own single malt whisky using another distillery, which offers far greater products. People at our clubs do not ask for Glenfiddich, and I make a pledge that no Trump property will ever do business with Glenfiddich or William Grant & Sons."

"I hereby call for a boycott on drinking Glenfiddich products because there is no way a result such as this could have been made by the Scottish people."

The orange toddler added that it was an insult to Scotland itself.

Does Trump actually believe that Scotland loves him? That William Grant & Sons would even have agreed to do a whisky with him? That the entire five million strong Scottish population adores him? Does he really believe that Glenfiddich would fix a people's vote result (as an aside, he may be recalling the time Diageo tried to steal an award BrewDog had legitimately won – and Diageo was unmercifully trolled once they got rumbled for it).

With 'I hereby call for a boycott on drinking Glenfiddich products' Trump attempted to wage war on the historic, deservedly-much-loved distiller. You just have to love the pompous, empirical use of 'hereby'. Did the people of Scotland who Trump says love him answer his battle call? Did they ever.

Bottles of Glenfiddich flew off the shelves in Aberdeenshire supermarkets, pubs and restaurants and so it proved throughout Scotland. The drink sold out in bars and restaurants. Menie residents were presented with bottles of the spirit as gifts. People who usually didn't drink whisky drank Glenfiddich, and some colourful toasts were made about Trump which are not quite suitable for publication.

As Severin Carrell wrote in his piece for the Guardian, the Glenfiddich team issued a calm, rational statement rather than sinking to Trump's level:

"Top Scot is a totally open category in which the people of Scotland can vote for whomsoever they choose and Glenfiddich has no influence on this decision. [The] Top Scot may be one of that year's category nominees or may come from any walk of life. The person receiving the greatest number of votes, cast by the people of Scotland, wins the award."

You could conclude from this that either the Russians and Cambridge Analytica interfered with this world-shakingly important vote and swung it for Michael Forbes, or that Trump is just not as deeply loved in Scotland as he tells us he is. Either way, the clear winners in this skirmish were Mr Forbes and Glenfiddich. Mr Forbes is still in his farm home, Glenfiddich sales have risen year on year, despite being spitefully banned from every Trump hotel and resort. A Glenfiddich executive confirmed to Aberdeen Voice the increase in sales; and they said this with a smile and a gleam in their eye.

It should be noted that a bottle of Trump-autographed whisky sold for £6,000 in an auction in 2017. No word yet on whether Glenfiddich's distillers are losing sleep at this development, but their turnover continues to grow. What that bottle may be worth in the future is another matter.

Still, if winning on this occasion meant for Trump that he successfully united thousands behind Michael Forbes, and his whisky ban made Glenfiddich have a huge sales spike while Trump himself looked like he'd been slapped in the face with a haddock, then he won. If that wasn't his intention, despite the amazing skills of Mr Sorial and despite Trump's larger-than-thou brain, he lost bigly.

If Sorial is to present a case to his readership that he and Trump were partners in winning, did Sorial have any involvement in the ridiculous statements and actions Trump put out? Wouldn't a canny lawyer have cautioned a client against attacking a loved Scottish institution like Glenfiddich? Either Sorial was not consulted on issues, or he approved of them.

3: Moving the goalposts: How Team Trump keeps changing the plan they were supposed to stick to – ongoing war

At the time of writing, March 2019, Aberdeenshire Council's planning officials recommended approval of Trump's revised plan to proceed with some 550 houses. This is a victory for Trump -- at the moment. The actual formal decision has been delayed – again. The battle may have gone to Trump, but the war is far from over.

Residents, concerned activists are beavering away on angles for opposing this development's development. The council, government agencies which should be proactively ensuring Trump sticks to the approved plan and the environment is safe seem to be cowering and burying their heads in the sand.

One of the Trump team's demands is to be allowed to do the

There are tales of people without Trump's clout who've fallen foul of planning, often innocently. The little guy funnily enough has virtually no chance of getting the planners to help them win retrospective planning permission. Trump's deliberately gone against the approved original plan at least a dozen times, and the response from planning is to give him retrospective permission.

The massive stone entrance with the giant Trump logo? As much as we all admire its tastefulness, it was not as per the approved plan. It stays put.

There is the giant, oversized flagpole. Some might think it is Trump's way of compensating for his little Super Mario mushroom cart. It stays put.

Whatever the satsuma statesman wants, he gets from Aberdeenshire Planning, or so it seems.

Back in March 2013 here's how planners responded to Aberdeen Voice on the matter:

"I acknowledge that the developer at the Menie Estate has, on a number of occasions, applied for planning permission which has been granted and subsequently the works that have been carried out are not in accordance with the approved plans. In all these instances the Planning Service has sought to address this situation by the submission of retrospective applications. Such applications are, unfortunately, relatively common where it has been identified that works have been undertaken in breach of planning control." - or in other words, while Mr Trump is supposed to stick to the plan as approved at national level, he doesn't have to.

There are people in Aberdeenshire made to tear down fences, walls, buildings, etc. because the council gave them a firm 'no' on their retrospective permission requests. They will be delighted to know the planners happily work with TIGLS to get any retrospective permissions needed. Who said there was one rule for the rich (well for Russian-funded developers anyway) and another for the poor? Actually, Andy Wightman said just that in his work 'The Poor Have No Lawyers' and anyone who wants background on how Scotland's once publicly-owned lands were carved up should read his book.

Aberdeen Voice wrote to planning numerous times, and got numerous deflections, half-answers and evasions. They once wrote:

"In the case of this development [Menie] I can assure you that it has been closely monitored. The Planning Service has followed up on all allegations of breaches of planning control including non-compliance with conditions or development which has been undertaken in breach of permission which has been granted... You have highlighted a number of other possible contraventions of planning permission at the Menie Estate and I will comment on these in turn..." (see Appendix I).

You may wonder what this monitoring is like if eleven or more pieces of work were not to the approved plan and were waived through retrospectively. They might have monitored, but they seem to have used Star Trek's Federation of Planet's 'Non-interference Directive' as a guide.

The email then goes through the eleven issues Aberdeen Voice raised; many of these were granted retrospective planning permission.

"I can assure you that Aberdeenshire Council and the Planning Service monitor this site and will continue to do so to ensure that works are carried out in accordance with the permissions granted [bang-up job so far] and to take necessary action where breaches occur [sure; like just granting retrospective permission]. The Service enforces planning and building regulations and access legislation in an equal and fair manner throughout the authority and all situations are dealt with in a consistent manner."

Or, in plain English Aberdeenshire planning admits TIGLS has on several occasions done what it wanted and got the council to fall in line after the fact.

This idea of taking 'necessary action where breaches occur' seems to mean the council grants Trump retrospective planning permission. Concerning the claim that planning is monitoring the site, the environmental monitoring group was merely allowed to fizzle out, and has not been reinstated (more on that elsewhere). No explanation for that is forthcoming, though Sorial once opined that MEMAG (Menie Environmental Monitoring Advisory Group) had done its job. The original condition was for 10 years of environmental monitoring to cover three phases of development. Does George not know this? More on MEMAG later.

Who are the people on the full council whose help past present and future Trump depends on? They include a councillor who allegedly asked Trump to donate to a charity they were connected to, a woman pleased to take Trump hospitality and be photographed grinning along with the Russia-linked magnate (granted – she's said she will not vote on Trump-related issues going forward), and although now retired, a man whose daughter worked directly for Trump, no mention of which ever managed to get on his register of interests. These people include some who have been called out over their pro-Trump posturing. If you were given a choice, Aberdeenshire Council or TIGLS: who would you say is in charge of how things are run at Menie

4. The Information Commissioner Wars:
Aberdeen Voice Victorious (sometimes)

Information is power. Whether you hold the footage (hypothetically speaking) of some pompous, overweight businessman having a Russian watersports session, or whether you hold data on how many millions of pounds a golf course is haemorrhaging per annum – facts rule the day. For logical, fair people anyway.

NB 'Information is not necessarily power in the more evangelically-inclined parts of America where white supremacy is taken as (part of the) Gospel, and the POTUS is deemed to have been chosen by God. Propaganda is more powerful than facts for some people who either chose or were indoctrinated into a state of ignorance. When the president says that Muller's 400 pages has exonerated him of wrongdoing or that wind power means you only have energy when the wind blows – there are those who will throw logic out of the window and believe him, sometimes verbally, physically abusing those who oppose their view. In more enlightened circles however, people actively look for information and present it to support their arguments.

Aberdeen Voice, Menie estate residents who oppose the suburbanisation of their environment, Anthony Baxter and others have actively sought facts to support a case against Trump continuing his campaigns at Menie. For their troubles they've occasionally had to pay with the occasional dubiously-legal arrest, name-calling by Sarah or Donald, 'accidental' power or water cuts and the like. The Trump organisation's spokesperson will put out any kind of drivel that is easily disproven – yet some papers print what she says without questioning her view. She says Scotland loves Trump and is earning money off the club: How many reporters are challenging these patently untrue statements?

However much the facts may make pro-Trump factions wince, they are facts. The place is losing money. They have not created a huge tourism increase. They have not created thousands of local jobs. It was off the back of these promises they were granted planning permission which overturned the SSSI designations and spelled the end for wildlife and the environment. Scotland does not universally love Trump. Far from.

Deer photographed jumping onto a Menie Estate road: how much time is left for the area's wildlife? 2013 S Kelly

Aberdeen Voice has often printed the unpalatable truths Aberdeen Journals Ltd (i.e. Bates) refused to. This book has hopefully given a flavour of these by now. Aberdeen Voice is tiny; it's run on donations, no one takes a salary (or has a Ferrari or Jimmy Choos). It takes articles from any side of an argument for publication as long as the facts check out and it is legal to publish it. AV has published the odd pro-Trump article or two – 100% of all pro-Trump articles submitted that passed a fact check were carried. You would think that Trump's Menie people might know who we are, but wouldn't stop to be troubled by small fry like us.

You would be wrong.

Rohan Beyts opening the floodgates on TIGLS's Information (mis) management at the estate (Ms Beyts was the lady an indignant, shocked Sarah Malone allegedly asked staff to film on their phones while she answered an urgent call of nature at the Estate in the sand dunes). Beyts' legal action against the unbelievable voyeuristic antics of TIGLS revealed that they had not, as demanded by law, set up any Data Protection systems. They blamed this on a clerical error. How an experienced project manager like Sarah Malone made this fundamental error is a mystery. As to golf courses, I have news for the dainty Mrs Bates: golfers have on occasion relieved themselves while out playing their 18 holes. Shocking I know. Not as shocking as allegations in Commander in Cheat by Rick Reilly on Trump's golf course antics, and claims Trump took a ten-year-old's golf ball to win a game, but shocking nonetheless.

Off the back of Beyts' revelations, I did a Subject Access Request for TIGLS to obtain any information it held concerning me. I thought for instance the attendees at the open house presentation on the proposed second course might have been videotaped, and that I might possibly have been recorded on other occasions. The reason I thought this was possible is that most times I've gone to the estate to visits the families or go for a walk, I am either watched by security in their vans or approached by course workers and questioned. The administration at Menie replied to my SAR to say no filming took place. And obviously I take them at their word, their filming of Beyts and security cars and vans notwithstanding.

However, Trump employees were bothered enough to visit my Facebook profile page on at least two occasions, copy my posts about the club, and discuss whether or not to take any action. Their own SAR response shows as much.

Did Aberdeen Voice, the mouse that roared, scare the yuge great elephant? It kind of looks that way.

The club redacted the names of TIGLS senders and recipients of the emails in question as expected. Their email accompanying their SAR report was marked PRIVATE & CONFIDENTIAL.

Naturally I quaked in my boots. Someone should have told them not only were they responsible for Data Protection from the start (they claimed they had just made an error – which is unlikely given Sarah's wide-ranging project management experiences and Cambridge degree) but that throwing 'Private and Confidential' on an email is a request you can make; it is not a mandatory directive for the recipient of such an email to follow (as long as they don't share any personal data without permission). Here, without revealing any of the protected personal data of any TIGLS personnel, are details of what I asked in my SAR, and how they responded.

I had asked a host of questions in my December 2016 cover letter; these went unanswered. Among those questions was a request for details on their excuse for not complying with data protection law; which TIGLS put down to some errant clerk:

"It is my understanding that 'clerical error' prevented your registration with the Scottish Information Commissioner before you began collecting data. Please advise exactly what happened – did you fill in registration forms and then a clerk forgot to lodge them? What error was a clerk meant to have made that prevented your legal and administration staff knowing TIGLS was not registered over the years? I understand you have 95 people in your employ; are many of these clerks? How many people are responsible for the overall management, and wouldn't any clerks' working fall under the remit of management? Thank you."

Shockingly, this question was not addressed in the TIGLS reply.

My SAR cover sheet is labelled with my name, email address and 'BLOGGER' - I like that. I'm no wordsmith like Damian Bates it's true, but I do have a few qualifications (a BA and MA in fine arts) up my sleeve and am an NUJ member (though

I never went to Cambridge like Mrs Bates did).

Here's some internal TIGLS correspondence from June 2016 unearthed by my SAR:

Hi, The following may be of Interest

This is taken from her Facebook timeline page.

"Suz still on Trump stuff, particularly in light of two Sarah Malone quotes. I am going to call her a liar in tomorrow's AV - or if it's too strong for AV, will do it as a personal blog. But the evidence is in. Malone quote 1 " I would categorically dispute any claims that we have purposely made life difficult for the neighbors or done things that were wrong." Quote 2: "We have a world-class developer whose brand is associated with luxury and excellence. I think he is a visionary, a very positive man. I can't work for someone I don't believe in." Comments please ladies and gentlemen - and feel free to add supporting instances."
Regards

In the line 'This is taken from 'her' Facebook timeline page,' the 'her' is me. The above refers to one of Malone's quotes that they've never done anything to make life difficult for the residents. This is obviously, patently not true, yet many members of the press just take quotes like this and run with them – when they could be asking David Milne about the fence and property damage, asking the Munros about the bunds and the damage done, or the Forbes who went without water while being called pigs. Journalists should be challenging obviously untrue statements, whoever issues them. Not doing so is how Trump bulldozes his way through obstacles such as laws and human rights.

Here is the second time that Trump's staff felt it necessary to act on the contents of my Facebook page from February 2016:

This is what Suzanne Kelly is saying on Facebook. Is it a joke or is Mr Trump due in Scotland on Saturday?

Well, I'm still busy with the Trump petition fallout, or I'd start another petition - besides, there's not much time before he plans to come to Scotland on Saturday. Instead, I'm writing to Teresa May, Police Scotland, and my MSPs /MPs. This clown has no business in Scotland. Maybe he'd like to talk to the Aberdeen rape support centre? Another talentless, damaged idiot trying to make a name for themselves by inflaming the public's outrage; straight out of the Katie Hopkins school of thought. write to your people here - https://www.writetothem.com/unless you think he's a 'free speech' champion

Now why would a billionaire's staff and lackeys be needing

to spy on a reporter – sorry blogger – like me if they didn't have something (or a whole barrelful of things) to fear? If someone called Sarah a liar and didn't have a legal leg to stand on, wouldn't Trump sue me?

I wouldn't have been baiting them about a potential Trump visit to see whether or not they were zooming me, would I (nudge nudge wink wink)? It did seem to create a bit of panic though.

The questions Team Trump left unanswered covered the environment, Susan Munro's cottage, Anthony Baxter's film, and many other issues. I guess they were too busy checking out my Facebook page to find time to answer. I am flattered; am thinking maybe dinner and a show.

Just a thought: What if the same energy applied to spying on a copiously-posting 'blogger' like yours truly was spent instead on attending environmental meetings or ensuring no 'clerical errors' derailed their data protection compliance? Perhaps things might be going a bit smoother at the complex? Not complying with well-publicised laws, harassing women and spying on people? This is hardly what anyone can call a win.

Now that that particular cat is out of the bag, it may almost seem superfluous to continue examining the wins and losses at Menie. Nevertheless, I will persevere.

5: More Facebook snooping - Shortbreadgate: a TIGLS Cock-up

It's bad enough that I suggested on my Facebook page that Drumpf might be flying in for a visit (as an aside, it's not particularly easy to find out how much these visits are costing the adoring Scottish taxpayer – but one cancelled visit cost at least £2,000 per a FOI request). However much Trump likes to say whatever pops into his big brain without regard for consequence; however much he wants his version of free speech at universities to the point of threatening federal funding cuts, TIGLS won't brook any self-expression of staff (or in this case staff's acquaintances) it doesn't like.

Mr President has just threatened universities with funding cuts if they curtail Freedom of Speech. No one in the White House had the impudence to point out that the First Amendment right carries with it a set of exemptions, or that hate speech is linked to increased violent crimes. Ironically, the free speech-loving Trump organisation is pretty keen to gag anyone who'd speak against it.

Someone at TIGLS seems to spend a great deal of time on social media whether spying on bloggers and journalists or ensuring staff stay in line. One Trump chef's Facebook profile page got him the sack.

The chef told the press that an acquaintance had put a photo of a shortbread that looked like a penis on the hapless cook's Facebook page. The chef was sacked immediately, and in trying to get back pay he claimed he was owed, he came to Aberdeen Voice for help – which we were happy to give him. Alas, while it seems he did get his full pay, it was conditional on him never speaking to the paper again, we understand.

There seems to be an obsession with things phallic in the Trump organisation. Giant flagpoles from Florida to Menie, oversized clocks on the Menie links (showing the incorrect time more often than not to people who have mobiles and wear Rolexes). And yet according to some (e.g. one Ms S Daniels), the President has a little tiny weenie button mushroom of a manhood. Perhaps the shortbread biscuit was somehow more phallic and more relevant on a chef's page than the phallic flagpoles and clocks dotting the course? A Freudian psychologist should be consulted.

The chef wasn't there when the biscuit was baked. He did not post the photo. As happens often, it was put on his Facebook home page by someone else. Ms Malone, unaccustomed to seeing this type of thing, was said to be apoplectic - a condition not foreign to her it seems.

They took him off the rota, and when he showed up for work and asked why, HR confronted him with page after page of screenshots printed from his Facebook account. Those free speech-loving Trump HR people don't like anyone exercising it when it doesn't go their way. He was fired over a biscuit someone else baked. The legality of this seems very dubious.

Whenever the news seems to be controversial, it's usually going to appear in the media tagged with 'a Trump spokesperson/ spokeswoman said' and not the Sarah Malone name. So it was with the Trump spokesperson's response as reported in the Daily Mail:

A spokesperson for Trump said: 'We make no apology for terminating the contracts of a number of individuals for gross misconduct on our property. ['on our property'? Did someone use her PC to post the shortbread pic? Do they own Facebook now?]

'We offer a world class service and customers in our hotel, restaurant and golf complex are our number one priority.

'We will not tolerate unprofessionalism of any kind and so we took immediate action to protect the interests of our business and guests."

Gross misconduct. Unprofessionalism. Amazing attention

to detail those Trump HR people have. If only the mechanic applied to the owners and high-ranking employees, not least certain security guards (more on that shortly). Mr Trump has been caught in thousands of lies according to the New York Times and other news outlets. He has called for violence against the press and others; he has insulted virtually every minority group there is. But the guests don't care about that – they would instead find out the names of the kitchen staff, google their social media, and freak out if they saw a shortbread that looked like a willie. Perhaps the cook already had a verbal and written warning? We may never know. But anyone who spends money at TIGLS or takes their charity is complicit in Trump's exploits.

In fairness, the world's greatest golf resort ever ever has to watch its fantastic reputation, or it could wind up losing its unrivalled Six Diamonds status. As every reader will know, this is the highest award a resort or hotel can get.

The well-known American Academy of Hospitality bestowed the coveted prize on Menie.

The prestigious Six Diamond award had never been achieved before; how thrilling is that?

For more details of what the award is about, a visit to the awarding body's website shows the Academy Trustees. The top row has a photo of one 'Ambassador Extraordinaire' – Donald Trump.

Precisely how the epic wins of maintaining the snow-white purity of TIGLS's reputation by firing the chef and winning the Six Diamonds will be covered in the Sorial/Bates book will be a delight to read. As to the untarnished, spotless moral reputation of Mrs Sarah Malone Bates, we should all aspire to such heights.

6: The Windfarms of War – Scotland's 'No' to Trump: Scotland wins

'Unsightly', 'disgusting looking', 'bad for people's health', enough to make someone "go crazy after a couple of years."

No, that's not what Scotland thinks of Donald J Trump. That's what Donald J Trump thinks of wind turbines.

View of offshore windfarms; clearly very distressing April 2019 (S Kelly)

The reason that there aren't more people golfing at TIGLS? It's not because of Trump links with racism, sexism, lying, his cutting medical aid to the poor, vilifying Mexicans and Muslims. It's because no one wants to look at an offshore windfarm while they are golfing.

Sadly, little evidence to back that claim has yet emerged. The proof for the Trump claim that electricity goes off when the wind doesn't blow is likewise not easily found. The newer claim Trump lodged that the noise from the turbines causes cancer oddly has not been backed by science as yet. Yet this man is keen to denounce CNN, The NY Times, etc as purveyors of 'Fake News.'

Mr Trump and Salmond famously fell out. Trump claimed Salmond promised that there would be no clean-energy-generating, job-creating offshore windfarms. Salmond says he made no such representation. Hard to know who to believe out of the two, but in this case, Salmond seems the more likely to be truthful.

Allowed to testify on the matter at Holyrood, Mr Trump and George A Sorial stumped up. Curiously, so did anti-wind farm protestors, some of whom say they were hired to be there. Who can ever forget Trump's masterful words to Parliament on the efficacy of wind power, and his expertise? When asked for evidence, the future president replied:

"I am the evidence."

Forget data suggesting man-made pollutants are exacerbating and accelerating climate change. Forget facts on renewable energy sector benefits. Trump embodies the evidence.

Trump's position as stated by factcheck.org:

"Clean power, right? They want to have windmills all over the place, right? When the wind doesn't blow, what do we do? Uh, we got problems. When there's thousands of birds laying [presumably big-brain meant lying] at the base of the windmill, what do we do? Isn't that amazing? The environmentalists, "We like windmills." Oh, really? What about the thousands of birds they're killing? Try going to the bottom of a windmill someday. It's not a pretty picture. But, really, when the wind doesn't blow, you got problems. If your house is staring at a windmill, not good. When you hear that noise going round and round and round, and you're living with it, and then you go crazy after a couple of years, not good. And the environmentalists say, oh, isn't it wonderful?"

Those kooky environmentalists.

Those who watched this historic moment live will long remember how proud, righteous and happy George looked to sit next to Donald; the men sported matching blue neckties. Some likened Sorial's face at the words 'I am the evidence' issuing from Trump's O-Ring shaped facial orifice to someone who's been hit in the face with a wind turbine blade. But the admiration Sorial has for the man with the evidence and the big brain was on show for all to see.

Not for the first time Scotland thwarted Trump. Despite his dragging the decision to proceed with the turbines through every court in the country, Drumpf lost. 'Loser' as he might say. Trump once said of the late Senator McCain – a man he can't stop insulting even after the veteran's death – 'he's no hero – I like heroes who don't get caught'. Trump is no hero rescuing us from the 'hell' of wind farm jobs and cleaner energy; he is in this case a huge loser who looks spectacularly uneducated (to those not in his fan club). The cost of this Scottish victory is to be borne by Mr Trump. No news reports have surfaced yet of his posting a cheque in the letterbox to Holyrood yet.

Will Mr Sorial tell his side of the story in his forthcoming compendium of wins? I am sure Damian Bates will agree that windfarms are bad, ugly inefficient things that kill birds by the thousands per turbine. The Scottish clean energy sector will be interested in how the decision resulting in hardship to traumatised rich golfers forced to look at rotating blades is worse than making clean energy and jobs.

Trump took out a newspaper advertisement on the subject of

wind farms; it showed a US highway with multiple wind farms and a picture of Alex Salmond. Linking in, as seems natural, the release of convicted Lockerbie Bomber al Megrahi to the issue, Trump's ad read:

"Tourism will suffer and the beauty of your country is in jeopardy! [written without a shred of irony or self-awareness]

"This is the same mind [Salmond's] that backed the release of terrorist al-Megrahi, 'for humane reasons' – after he ruthlessly killed 270 people on Pan-Am Flight 103 over Lockerbie" [if there were prizes for tenuous links, this would win something major].

Twenty-one people complained formally to the Advertising Standards Agency about this dog's dinner of a page spread. Among those having none of it was the Green Party's Patrick Harvie MSP, who said:

"Trump has sunk to a new low. Linking renewables policy to Lockerbie victims is sick.

Not only did he have no shred of evidence that tourism would suffer when we quizzed him during the parliament's inquiry into renewables, he has already been censured by the authorities for placing similar anti-renewables adverts.

Trump's organisation has already trashed a unique environment on the coast of Aberdeenshire and trampled on the rights of local people. Now he appears to be determined to buy up chunks of the Scottish press. It's vital that Scotland doesn't allow a bully to think he can flash his cash and get his own way."

If Trump were trying to send a message to Scots that windfarms were bad because Salmond was in favour of them and Salmond's release of al-Megrahi proved Salmond was wrong, it didn't seem to work. Trying to manipulate the Scottish people by this heavy-handed, bizarre ad did not exactly get people in the streets rallying for Trump. As an aside not everyone is 100% convinced al Megrahi was the true and/or sole culprit; this includes some Lockerbie families. Anyone wanting to know more could do worse than read Private Eye's special report, 'Lockerbie: The Flight from Justice'.

Doubtless a canny billionaire would check any ad campaigns with his team. Mr Sorial said this on the matter according to edie.net in December 2012:

"The Green Party's policies should be challenged on every front because they have done nothing to protect the deliberate mutilation of their own environment, coastline and countryside. Members of "green" groups must be embarrassed.

"Those who lost a family member or a friend in the Lockerbie tragedy must be incredibly incensed with Alex Salmond for releasing a murderous criminal."

Residents and frequent visitors to the estate report the turbines have had no discernible impact on the paltry number of cars they usually see in the parking lot.

How the ad ever got published is a fair question; it has clearly wild assertions about wind farms ruining tourism; its use of al Megrahi to ham-fistedly try to foment hate for Salmond, etc would have had most papers reject it outright. So which papers did run it? You might be able to guess one.

Aberdeen Journals Ltd.'s Press and Journal was one paper to take the ad; the other, The Courier, has the same owners as the Piss n Churnal – D C Thomson.

Not really deserving of a chapter of its own, but of possible related interest is the Press & Journal's handling of advertising for Anthony Baxter's third documentary, 'You've Been Trumped Too'. On the back of the previous award-winning documentaries, this film was released at Cineworld theatres, quite an accomplishment for a documentary.

When the Press & Journal published its list of upcoming movies, an Aberdeen Voice reporter noticed the film's absence from the Cineworld listings. Unable to get a straight answer as to why this should be, the reporter (me) wrote and placed a classified ad in the paper to announce the film; this was done over the internet. Shortly after doing so, the reporter got a call from the paper's classified ads team to say the ad would not be carried because my announcement didn't really fall into the 'announcements' category.

Amazing how the vetting of ads can vary within one regional newspaper, isn't it? Undaunted, I told them that unless the movie was included in the next published list of cinema releases, I would write an article for Aberdeen Voice on the absence of the film from the paper Mr Bates edited, and send the story to other UK papers.

The ad appeared, just as the wind farms have appeared offshore from Menie.

Finally, these Trump 'winners' used one of their ancient playbook techniques: they hired people to protest wind turbines being built (yes, really). The rent-a-mob came from university students and others desperate to make a quid or two. It seems Trump embodying the evidence and linking wind farms with bombing wasn't considered a strong enough winning hand.

The Mirror reported that students said they had been paid £20 per hour and given signs to hold up; one student said the hired mob rather lacked enthusiasm for the work.

It might seem kind of a cheeky, funny prank- hiring protestors for Holyrood and giving them signs and money – the Trump team deny this despite the witnesses' claims to the contrary. However, Trump really did say this to the Irish Times: "Wind farms are a disaster for Scotland, like Pan Am 103."

Whoever in the Drumpf organisation is responsible for checking its advertisements and media statements for truth clearly has no ethics filter. Whoever is allowing the vermillion beast to place ads that the regulator has to ban, hires protestors, and clears statements linking terrorism and cancer to wind farms may eventually figure out the tactics that might fool some ignorant Americans have backfired in Scotland – spectacularly.

7: The Bunker – Enemy Stronghold on Trump's Estate: Drumpf Loses

Any general worth his salt knows that if the enemy holds territory within your borders and are entrenched, you've got a problem. Trump, Bates and Malone-Bates have problems.

As well as their utter failure to persuade Menie families to sell up (be it to Trump or Trump's lackey larping as a tourist looking to buy a home), the bunker is a further complication.

What is the bunker? It is a plot of land in the middle of Trump's Menie estate that legally is owned by people – lots of them. Thousands.

Lord Puttnam, famed for his prescient film Local Hero, is one of the owners of this little acre that remains a headache for TIGLS. As far as I understand it, getting a clear title on this little acre, let alone doing a compulsory purchase may prove too much even for a winner like lawyer Sorial, when he was still on the case.

This is what TUT says about the bunker:

"The Tripping Up Trump campaign acquired some land right at the heart of Donald Trump's planned private housing and leisure development. The reason TUT has done this is to help protect the families who have forced eviction (by means of Compulsory Purchase Orders) hanging over their heads. The families of Menie have again and again stated they do not wish to leave but still Trump and Aberdeenshire Council won't withdraw the threat of using CPOs if the families don't agree to sell 'voluntarily'.

Worse still, the families have been harassed and lied to from day one. Donald Trump received outline planning permission claiming he had all the land he needed. Once his planning permission was granted, he suddenly changed his mind and approached Aberdeenshire Council for help with his bid to take possession of his neighbours' land and homes.

Tripping Up Trump has 60 new landowners and is offering anyone who wants to help defend the Menie families the opportunity to join us and become 'One of Menie'. You will eventually be added to the deeds of The Bunker, helping to make the option of Compulsory Purchase Orders close to impossible for Aberdeenshire Council and the Trump Organisation."

There is an element of relief to be gained from the recent statement from Donald Trump regarding his decision not to use Compulsory Purchase Orders in relation to his housing development here at Menie. However, the statement has been treated with scepticism by myself and many others simply because in his statement he claims never to have actually requested CPOs in the first place, this is untrue.

The letters show quite clearly that a formal request for CPOs to be used was made on March 4, 2009 and was the result of some considerable prior discussion. Therefore, until such time a formal letter withdrawing the request is made public, this application can be reinstated at any time."

Councillors Martin Ford, Paul Johnston and then Councillor Debra Storr actively fought against the threat of compulsory purchases, a very real worry which hung over the families' heads for many years unnecessarily. Aberdeen Voice has yet to find evidence of former Councillor Tom Malone similarly fighting to prevent Aberdeenshire citizens facing a US billionaire turfing them out of their homes

An attempt at denying CPOs were ever requested was dealt a fatal blow by David Milne; he shared a letter proving the TIGLS threat was very real. For some odd reason, Mr Milne decided to share this scoop with Aberdeen Voice rather than the Press and Journal.

How it must rankle. There are some things and some people that just cannot be bought and who will not bow down to wealth, fame and power. Go figure.

Should you ever find yourself wandering over the golf course at Menie, while stopping to wipe the blue-green powdery chemicals from the grass off your shoes – look up. If you see a Mexican flag flying in the middle of what seems like nowhere, you've found the bunker. It is a tribute to the creative protesting of Tripping up Trump, it is the stone in Trump's shoe and the fly in his ointment. It is glorious.

8: The Resistance -- Tripping up Trump

"'We stood and we are ready to stand' is the motto of Tripping up Trump, the organisation standing against Trump's plans for the Menie Estate." – Tripping up Trump http://www.trippinguptrump.co.uk

Despite Mr Bates pronouncing that the group is not 'bona fide' (and he should know if something is genuine or not, being a former newspaper editor beyond reproach), the group meets, communicates with its members, has social media presence, and has successfully annoyed the opposition.

Its web page banner reads: "A popular movement against using compulsory purchase for private profit". As previously discussed, the truth of Trump's seeking CPOs was broken in an Aberdeen Voice article by David Milne, that Trump definitely sought to get compulsory purchase orders against those who would not sell up to him. In Scotland such orders are infrequently used and apply to government projects of huge importance such as airport and highway construction. Trump should know from his love of Scotland that a very dim view is taken of trying to throw people out of their homes for the rich. Perhaps Sarah should explain the Highland Clearances to Trump; with her educational background she'll be well placed to explain the historic socio-economic factors and why rich people throwing poor ones out of their homes is likely to sit badly with many Scots.

Attempts were made to infiltrate Tripping Up Trump's membership both online and as is suspected at meetings. This should not shock anyone; the police in the UK have infiltrated all sorts of legal protest groups from 'Reclaim the Streets' to grassroots environmental campaigns. Anyone wanting details of the infuriating, illegal, immoral way in which police officers took the identity of dead children and set up false identities in order to seduce and even impregnate female protestors should look into the wonderful work being done by Police Spies out of Lives.

Occasionally new members on TUT's social media have suggested violence and vandalism and tried to incite it. Such people are thrown out swiftly. It is a non-violent group relying on witty and dignified protests.

Members come from all over the place, including Glasgow (which for some reason bothered Damian). An American whose sons are quoted as saying Russian money will be used to build on the country's only moving sand dune system didn't bother Damian, but the prospect of a Glaswegian commenting on their country's environmental heritage did. I think we should be told what the ex-newsman uses as a yardstick. This group has had some spectacular victories; something that must bother their wealthy, connected opponents greatly. Tripping up Trump can be found at http://www.trippinguptrump.co.uk .

9: War of words: name calling – Trump dishes it out; Scotland replies in spades

'Miss Housekeeping' – or Alicia Machado as she is better known, gained weight and the ever fit, svelte Donald Trump dubbed her 'Miss Piggy'. The bully does like monikers: 'Crazy Bernie', 'Little Adam Schitt', 'Cheatin' Obama' – you get the idea. The NY Times counted 567 insults Trump's hurled at people.

When Drumpf started insulting Menie Residents, Scotland answered. Michael Forbes lived, according to Trump, in 'a pigsty' (it's a charming, working farm by the way) and was accused of verbally agreeing to sell (as if) to Trump but then backed out.

As well as electing Forbes the Top Scot of 2012, the Scots came up with some epithets for Donald as only they can.

Placards at anti-Trump demonstrations have called Donald 'Ya radge orange bampot', 'mangled apricot hellbeast', 'Bawbag-eyed f**k bumper', and the succinct 'c*nt' as seen on a protest sign that's become rather iconic.   If Scotland loves the man as he claims, it's looking like one of those 'love/hate' kind of affairs.

Name calling may be immature, but like satire, it is a weapon against the powerful the otherwise powerless can use. When governments local and national are not going to enforce the law, or enforce it subjectively, some will fight back in every non-violent way possible as they've done since the time of the Romans. And the Romans have done a lot more for us than Trump has.

The next time Trump pronounces 'Scotland Loves me!' – just remember – most Scots think of him as a 'Toupéd f**ktrumpet' and/or Hamster heedit bampot.

10: Forth Estate or Fifth Column? P&J battle – Rumbled

Mr Bates' stewardship of Aberdeen Journals Ltd is the stuff of fairytales. He found his fair princess, he made his fortune. And he's hanging with the President.

Jealousy is such an ugly thing. Not only has the P&Poo taken a few hits in the Aberdeen Voice, but Private Eye has also questioned the paper's ethics, and rudely referred to the 45th President of the United States as a 'bewigged megalomaniac'.

Perhaps we are all just jealous of not having access to those Trump press conferences or hanging at the White House. It was once suggested that I was just jealous of these people – presumably of their wealth and power. I can promise you, I'm really not.

Before going into some of the papers' finer pro-Trump moments, a question: if Donald J Trump has successfully been isolated from his former businesses by the sterling efforts of compliance guru George Sorial, then why was Damian Bates hanging at the White House at all? More on that shortly.

Why would anyone think the august Press & Journal and its little sister the (very) tabloid Evening Express had a hint of pro-Trump bias? There are clues.

The 'slice of heaven' clubhouse February 2013; oozing luxury and class according to some (S Kelly)

<u>Evening Express</u>

"This slice of heaven really is worth the trip." – unnamed Evening Express Reporter, 26/04/2015

"We turned up at the clubhouse – where The Brasserie is based – to warm welcomes and smiling faces, even from the staff in the golf shop. [smiling faces at a five-star/six-diamond resort - even from the shop staff! Fancy!]

"We were early for our 2pm reservation – having finished a walk nearby quicker than we had anticipated – but despite that we were instantly offered a table or a hot drink [was that either a table or a hot drink as the prose implied – couldn't the writer have both?] in a room adjoining the restaurant that was full of comfy couches [as opposed to all those uncomfortable couches you find in hotels]. ["Restaurant offers hot drinks shocker"]

"We gladly accepted a hot tea and coffee (which came with a delicious piece of shortbread) and settled back to relax before our late lunch.

The decor was luxurious without being too over the top and was extremely comfortable and the waiters were attentive without bothering us too much." – Jennifer Buchanan, 28/2/2016

The Evening Express is the quasi-red-top, little sister to the Press & Journal; surely the P&J would have more measured, objective reporting on the Trump facilities? 'Would it? – F**k' to use a traditional Scottish expression.

"We were luxuriating in those delicious moments before sliding from reality into the twilight zone of dreamland, when it suddenly dawned on me that I was sharing Donald Trump's bed." Wrote David Knight in February 2016 [omg did he get sick and/or freak out?];

"My wife and I were enjoying a preview of the Valentine's treats on offer here next weekend. If you are looking for opulence and luxury, fine food, an intimate setting – and being treated like a lord and lady – you cannot go wrong with MacLeod House, the gem in Mr Trump's estate and golf resort, Trump International links, near Balmedie…"

The 'article' finished with an advertisement for your £295 Valentines escape to TIGLS. Hard-hitting reporting like this is a treat.

11: War on Journalism: – Trump attacks the Media while Bates shares photos of Air Force One – Is this an own goal?

As alluded to before, you have to hand it to Master Bates: he's an ex newspaper man about to launch a homage to a man who has waged a war on the press that has got people killed, but Bates still is on board with Trump. That's some precarious position to choose.

Four journalists were shot dead in Maryland by an extreme right winger; Trump has called the press 'The Enemy of the People' (does that have a familiar ring to it?). Far right-wing zealots are pitched as 'journalists' (Milo and his ilk) while respected, international news-gathering media outlets are ridiculed.

As explained earlier, Bates, undeterred, posted photos on Facebook of himself standing in front of the White House and the presidential plane: what official US Government business does he have? More to the point – what respect for other journalists does he have?

Was he there because of the amazing international reach of the Aberdeen Evening Express? Did the piece in the P&J

about the lost cow capture America's heart? Or, since Drumpf has been in the White House for two years, and the photo of Damian was clearly taken after Trump had access to Air Force One and the White House: is it still a remote possibility that some overlap remains between the presidency and the president's former business interests? If the two things were kept separate by former compliance guru Sorial, then why was Damian there? When Mr Sorial answers Aberdeen Voice's questions asked by email before his departure from the Trump organisation, this book will be updated in order to put all our minds to rest. But I wouldn't hold your breath for the revised edition to come out any time soon.

An Aberdeen Voice article about Damian Bates' social media record reflecting his proximity to the White House and Air Force One is being read in locations including Washington DC and by people a stone's throw from Mar-a-Lago. Maybe someone in a position of power will look into whether or not this is, as it looks to many, a breach of the emoluments clause. Coincidentally, it was not long after the AV article questioning the robustness of White House adherence to the emoluments clause appeared that Mr Sorial bowed out.

When a newspaper in Scotland invites one presidential candidate to write an 'exclusive' column for the paper – what does that say (Bates' organs didn't carry any columns from Clinton)? DC Thompson is not run by idiots (probably); they are aware of the mountain of evidence proving Trump's history of bigotry, sexism and lying. They must have known Bates had the massive conflict of interest in that half of his family's breadwinners works for Trump. Why did they want their paper to go to the far right of the presidential debate? Are they that desperate for advertising revenue from the kumquat they would sell their souls and hoodwink their readership? Should DC Thomson respond, it will be included in the next edition of this book.

Things are rapidly changing in journalism; a Milo or a Katie can earn a tonne of money by writing inflammatory, outrageous xenophobic pieces. The P&J and EE can sell copies by including 'exclusive' Donald Trump columns despite his mocking a NYT journalist and denouncing the profession. It seems hate sells. Things are badly broken, and some people would rather court racists than try to fix what's going wrong.

The biggest UK attack on the freedom of the press came with the arrest of Anthony Baxter and Richard Phinney though. The National Union of Journalists were rightly angry over the unprecedented move.

The Guardian reported:

"Paul Holleran, the NUJ's regional organiser in Scotland, said the arrests were unjustified and had important implications for press freedom. A formal letter of complaint has been sent to the Grampian chief constable, Colin McKerracher.

"'This is a blatant example of police interference aimed at stopping bona fide journalists from doing their job," Holleran said.

Their footage shows they were asking very pertinent questions in a mannerly fashion as befits professional journalists. I believe this is a breach of human rights, and we are taking legal advice. I think this must be one of the first cases in this country of journalists being arrested for just carrying out interviews to establish the truth and hold people to account."

If Bates ever joined the outcry against the police suppression of journalists, no trace of it has been found.

12: Your Own Private Police Force: What Every Dictator Wants – Trump Riles Scotland

The policing policy for the estate started out as a Trump victory at the expense of local people, journalism and the right to roam. It seems even the police are sick of Trump today, but the past tells a different story.

Trump was not president when he bought Menie; he was not a presidential candidate; he was not involved in politics. He was a millionaire (allegedly) with a dubious history involving bankruptcies best known for saying 'you're fired' on a bitchy, exploitative television show. He was a known associate of underworld figures. Therefore, Grampian police decided to invent a new, rights-busting policing strategy for his estate.

Persuaded somehow that his property was going to be the object of vandalism, the police (then Grampian Police, later absorbed in Police Scotland) put in place a bespoke policy for the estate. Some minor vandalism did happen according to Trump; Trump's teams however vandalised residents' property when they cut water, broke items at the Milne's home, etc. The police explained:

"...in Spring 2009, following the announcement of a number of strategic economic and infrastructure developments, Grampian Police established a short life Critical Incident Preparation Group (CIPG).

... a generic, local strategy, relevant to Menie Estate (was) developed. This has been determined as; Maximise safety; minimise disruption; facilitate lawful protest; deter, detect, detain and report those responsible for unlawful behaviour."

It is hard to see how in practice this was a two-way street. Trump's builders 'accidentally' broke the water pipe supplying the Forbes farm and did not restore it – no police action.

Anthony Baxter and Richard Phinney, who went to the site office to ask about this, then were arrested a short time later for a 'breach of the peace' – their equipment seized and they were put in cells.

Trump's operatives removed property and broke property when erecting a fence with no consultation on the Trump/ Milne border – the offences were caught on video by David Milne: nothing at all was done about it; the police had the tape proving the vandalism and they were not interested. Justice is neither as blind nor as just as she used to be.

Trump's security guard screamed at photographer/ photojournalist Alicia Bruce, threatening that he would 'smash up her camera.' He was so threatening she called for police help and called her partner. The police on learning a male security professional threatened Ms Bruce... actively dissuaded her from pressing charges.

As already mentioned elsewhere, Trump's people planted border flags in Mr Forbes' field – where there were equines which would have easily been injured if they had stepped on one – he removed them. He was promptly arrested and cautioned. The flags, which he had no idea how they came to be in his field, and which he had no desire to keep, were worth £11. (Seriously, what is it with Trump and flags?).

Trump locked off the path from the Forbes' Farm to the water where Michael used to take his salmon boat to fish at sea; police told Forbes that (despite the path being used for decades) he would be promptly arrested if he touched the gate or the lock.

Gate off Leyton Farm Road with sign warning of CCTV surveillance; pity no one at the time had checked in with the Information Commissioner due to a 'clerical error' (S Kelly)

Maybe it's a good thing Grampian Police has been subsumed into Police Scotland; if it spells the end of a local thuggery in uniform bullying journalists and residents, and looking the other way when it suits them - great.

[I have tried to keep references from Aberdeen Voice to a minimum in this book, but this situation still angers me – see Appendix IV if interested in more details, how the Information Commissioner acted when we tried to get information on policing].

Policing is not without its financial cost, however zealous those deployed at Menie were to arrest reporters yet ignore select criminal activity. Aberdeen Voice managed to find out that the cost of one cancelled Trump visit to the area exceeded £8,000 – we wonder what it costs every time a Trump dynasty member flies in for a round of golf or to talk to councillors and planners. The BBC reported that Trump's visit to May in July of 2018 cost £5 million. When it comes to the promise the magnate made of creating jobs, maybe it was policing jobs he meant.

As to doing freedom of information requests on the police, Aberdeen Voice has had a colourful time to put it mildly, but that is for another time. Suffice it to say that they once lost a case file into property dealings by Aberdeen City Council that Audit Scotland could not figure out constituted fraud or incompetence, and another time Police Scotland held an internal enquiry on an AV FOI request but later derailed an Information Commissioner request when they later decided they had been wrong to hold the enquiry.

13: War Of The Bunds – A Trump Win - But Another Public Relations Loss

Leyton Cottage has huge kitchen windows. In the past the Munro family would look out these windows and be able to see miles of unspoilt coastal land; sun would stream in. They also have a bench on their land they used to sit on and look at the sea. They can forget about that view now, too.

Trump decided he would shield the sensitive eyes of his golfers by building a giant mount of steep sand and dirt between the cottage and the sea. Now the Munros see this mound instead of anything else – and the council seems to be fine with that.

The council, which promised its personnel were on site inspecting and ensuring compliance were happy for these mounds – bunds – to exceed 6' in height and for the sand and dirt to blow in to the Munro house, garden and cars with impunity. Car engines were damaged, many plants died, the dirt blew into their home.

Section of the bund (right side of photo) – mound of earth and sand planted to 'screen' the Munro home, i.e. taking away the family's view across the land and sea,

October 2014 (S Kelly)

Ms Malone said words to the effect that if they are going to live near a construction site, they should expect this. At one point Sarah tried the friendly approach, and would invite Susan to lunch or tea, knowing full well the family were not going to sell. Susan refused, despite the 'luxurious' settings the Press & Journal reporters(?) raved about and Mrs Malone-Bates' warmth and charm.

Things are now at a bizarre impasse: Trump, the council, and 'environmental consultant' Ironside Farrar seem to be claiming the bunds have all been reduced to 1.5 metre in height. As no dirt was removed, no bulldozers deployed and the mounds still tower over visitors, no one understands this claim. The council put it in an email, and Ironside Farrar wrote in a report:

On 13 June 2013, Aberdeenshire Council granted planning permission for the construction of amended design proposals for the carpark to service the Championship Golf Course and Golf House at the Menie Estate (Ref: F/APP/2012/2342). This planning permission is the subject of four planning conditions, the first of which states that:

1   An amended plan, to include details of the reduction in height of the bunding to 1.5 metres and removal of the 3 lighting columns immediately adjacent to the boundary with Leyton Cottage, as specified, shall be submitted within 1 month for the approval of the Planning Authority. Thereafter and within 2 months of the date of the decision hereby approved, the bund shall be re-profiled in accordance with the approved plans and the lighting columns removed. In addition, the Pine trees planted on the top of the bund shall be removed and only native shrub planting shall be planted on the east side of the bund, there shall be no planting on the west side or on top of the bund at any time.

   Reason: To ensure the implementation of a satisfactory scheme of landscaping which will help to integrate the proposed development into the local landscape in the interest of the visual amenity of the area.

With the mound reduced in height to 1.5m, Leyton Cottage, including the dormer window in the roof, is clearly visible from the Golf House carpark. This in turn means that the Golf House carpark, including the carpark lighting, is clearly visible from the upper storey of Leyton Cottage, to the detriment of the visual and residential amenity of the owner/occupier of the property.

The Design Proposals

The design proposal comprises a screen mound 2.5m in height with an undulating ridge top to reflect the local dune landscape of the raised beach. The height of 2.5m is determined by the requirement to screen views, from the dormer window in the roof, of the Golf House carpark. As the carpark is 175m in length running east from the boundary with Leyton Cottage, the mound at 2.5m will ensure that the majority of the carpark and lighting will not be visible from Leyton Cottage. This will in turn protect the residential amenity of the owner/occupier of the property.

The council briefly covered the subject (Appendix I) to say the bunds were on the original plan (some dispute this); the council agreed the bunds were higher than planned. What precisely happened to the claim the bunds were reduced to 1.5 metres is another mystery, but the council granted retrospective planning permission for them. Aberdeen Voice saw the bunds when they were new; they saw them again in April of 2019: they have not been reduced as far as we can see. So much for local government looking out for the interests of residents over developers which overstep their approved plans.

The Scottish reporters' permission for this preposterous venture said that there should be no deviation from the approved plan.

It looks as if no one locally or nationally is stepping up to the plate to ensure compliance; TIGLS is doing as it pleases.

Interim Solution

As an interim measure, the landscape mound has been reduced in height to 1.5m, the trees and shrubs removed and the mound dressed in turf. In addition, the three lamp standards adjacent to the boundary with Leyton Cottage have been removed.

Precisely who at the council received this report and agreed to its contents has not been discovered. The family were not consulted by Ironside Farrar. The Munros did not want to be 'protected' from looking out to sea. The bunds have not been reduced, and the idea of 'matching the dunes' – which are a good distance away, is rubbish.

Aberdeen Voice lodged a complaint about this to the firm and a regulatory body Ironside Farrar belongs to, and is meant to adhere to its code. No answers were forthcoming.

Does my bund look big in this? Section of Bund near the Munro's property: I'm 5' 9 ½".

Does this bund look like it's under 6' to you? " Photo by Fred Wilkinson 2019

14: The Secret Weapon: Anthony Baxter – Trump utterly discredited

No journalist has done as much for the Menie Estate and its long-suffering residents than Anthony Baxter, director of You've Been Trumped, A Dangerous Game, and You've Been Trumped Too.

He and partner Richard Phinney created three award-winning documentaries showing what life is like on the estate for the Munro, Milne and Forbes families. Their trilogy of films shown the sensitive environment bulldozed and the bunds built. Baxter and Phinney were arrested after interviewing – with permission – the site office manager about the Forbes' water supply, as already covered; the film shows a calm pair of journalists being confronted by a seriously angry site manager and later a seriously agitated policeman.

Re-mortgaging his home to help raise funds, Baxter has been relentless. He has well and truly been a thorn in the sides of Trump and Malone.

His third film was rushed out in a hurry – he wanted to show it to as many people as possible before the presidential elections. It was made available on social media, and is highly recommended.

At the after party for the second film, held at Aberdeen's Café 52, residents mingled with journalists and supporters.

Cake for the party based on one of the film's promo posters (made by, photographed by and eaten by S Kelly)

On the occasion of the film premier and party, a person we will call AG involved in a number of local charities and good causes told guests how the pro-Trump camp tried and failed to get him on side with the Trump project. They even brought out the big guns.

One day AG received a call from The Donald himself. Donald went into the details of the course, and AG told him in no uncertain terms he was against it. Donald continued to argue the case, and eventually an exasperated AG simply said he had to go and hung up.

In the wee hours of the night that call took place, the AG residence's phone rang. Answering it half asleep, AG was astonished to find a ranting, raving, furious Trump on the other end.

"No one hangs up on Donald Trump! NO ONE!!!" the belligerent billionaire bellowed down the line at an astonished but sleepy AG.

AG again hung up. The guests at the party for Baxter's film had a good laugh, but were not surprised.

Have Aberdeenshire council, central government, any of the environmental agencies taken heed of the films or asked Anthony for any further details of what he's uncovered? Did Damian Bates launch his own investigation? Certainly not. Nothing proactive that might favour the residents or the environment takes place as far as can be determined.

Baxter was instrumental in getting the USA's media to take a closer look at Menie. The first time his first film was shown in Aberdeen, Menie residents attended, and so did I. Talking to Anthony and the residents that day is the reason Aberdeen Voice contributors and TUT members have tried to help.

Anyone wanting to find out what's going on in Aberdeen could do worse than visit Café 52; many journalists from all over the world have stopped in now, for choice quotes, updates and good food and drink.

The proprietor was asked by a Mashables reporter for a quote when the UK hate speech petition was live. Mashables wrote this about the encounter:

"His (Café 52's owner) views on Donald Trump don't leave much room for interpretation.

"'He's a c*nt," he says. "You don't come to Scotland and treat people like shit, take people's homes away and you don't destroy the Scottish landscape.'"

What would Dear Donald's Scottish mother say?

15: Sorial Triumphant? Trump's Top Tweets – May Yet Explode

What could possibly go wrong under the stewardship of George A Sorial, the man who was until recently in charge of compliance for Donald J Trump? Answer – almost everything.

Leaving aside for the moment the questions over emolulments, conflicts of interest, and compliance, Trump will be forever remembered for his tweets. Who can forget his kindly words to Senator McCain's family, his refusal to believe white terrorism is on the rise (or that he has any part in it), and the nice things he's tweeted about those who don't agree with him?

Perhaps his tweet to the UK suggesting it should appease him has slightly crossed some of those emoluments clause, ethics and dignity lines George was meant to be managing.

Telling Trump not to tweet must be rather like giving a child a box of crayons and telling it not to use them. In fact, crayons might have been a good suggestion.

Here's what Trump tweeted on 2 March 2019 from his official presidential account, and what some of the press makes of it.

"Very proud of perhaps the greatest golf course anywhere in the world. Also, furthers U.K. relationship!"

Trump was retweeting this from The Trump Organization:

"The landscape framework of @TrumpScotland comes close to an ideal. There is nothing missing & there are no weak holes [no, no weak holes, just the one that fell into the sea after a storm]." Dr. Martin Hawtree http//:TrumpGolfScotland.com "

What's wrong with that you might wonder. Firstly, Trump was supposed to, with Sorial's expert guidance, ensure there were no overlaps between the office of the presidency and Trump's business interests (his name may no longer be on the Companies House documents for Menie or Turnberry, but his immediately family run them). Secondly, Trump's Menie club is trying to get the planning conditions watered down so they can build more cheaply than was agreed, as earlier written.

Therefore, suggesting that the USA's relationship with the UK is in any way furthered by the Menie course is in simplified legal terms – simply not on.

Mother Jones' headline of March 5 2019 sums the situation up:

"Was Trump Threatening Our UK Allies With This Tweet About His Scottish Golf Course?

"He 'explicitly and deliberately tied the fate of his Scottish golf club to the UK/US Special Relationship'."

The Daily Record did a nice headline too for a piece by John Niven:

"Donald Trump is engaging in a Mafia-style threat to Scotland - and Nicola Sturgeon should sue"

Whether it was more of a defenestration or more like a rat jumping ship, George A Sorial was gone within a few weeks of that headline. What happened to end his career helping Trump 'win'? We should be told, but I suspect we won't be.

16: Forbes family – An 80-Something -Year-Old Woman Is Stronger Than Trump

A farmer, his wife, his mother, lots of cats and chickens and other animals are in Trump's way at Menie. He's tried ridiculing them in the press, his lackeys accidentally (?) cut their water supply. He's stopped them crossing his land as they had for years to go salmon fishing. They've seen arrests and cautions from a police force that otherwise were bungling cases (elsewhere unlawfully taking DNA swabs for one). He's tried disputing land boundaries and had the farmer arrested for moving the flags his people planted without warning. The farmer, Michael Forbes, his wife Sheila and mother Molly are still there. Trump must absolutely hate this.

At the Forbes property (S Kelly)

There's one law for Trump and another for people like Michael Forbes. Imagine coming home and finding in a field where you keep equines a series of small flags – flags which could seriously harm a horse's hooves and legs if they stood on them. Not knowing how they got there or why, you collect them. The police promptly show up and arrest you for 'theft' of the flags on your property: flags worth £11. Property disputes are normally a civil matter – but those £11 flags – that was enough to get the police involved. Consider that next time you need a swift response to a stolen bicycle, vandalised car or break-in.

Compare and contrast with what the Trump organisation did to David Milne. They went on his land, broke property, erected a fence in an area that's disputed, and sent him a bill for £3k. Did the police do anything about the trespass or damaged property? Of course not.

The police and the council didn't take any such proactive action to restore the Forbes' water supply; they were aware that Molly, in her 80s, had to fetch water for her chickens, her bathing and her cooking from a nearby stream. You can imagine what would have been done to Mr Forbes had he accidentally broken a water supply to Tump considering his arrest over the boundary flags.

A Forbes Farmyard conference (S Kelly)

Just as was done to the journalists, Forbes was cautioned that if he breached the peace again, he would be in legal trouble. This breach of the peace law seems to be used to control and to gag. Baxter wanted his day in court; before he got the chance, the police simply dropped the charges, which still meant Baxter had to 'behave' and never got to tell a court his side. The law needs changing and the police who abuse it need to face charges for doing so. Who actually was pulling the police's strings at the time is what we need to know, but may never find out.

Trump decided to sue the family, this being one of the biggest

101

bullying tools in the arsenal of a multi-millionaire: to threaten someone with a lawsuit they cannot possibly pay for. With the prospect of getting legal aid in the UK recently made far more difficult and unlikely, this must have been some worry. The cause? Molly's home is a temporary building. Trump's own 'temporary' giant marquee on the estate (very classy) seems to have stayed up longer than it was meant to, but no one threatened to sue him. You might ask yourself what kind of 'winner' threatens the home of a woman in her 80s, what kind of lawyer would happily follow orders to carry out such an instruction, and what kind of newspaper person would defend the millionaire over the residents of the paper's catchment area. You have the answer: a guy who would cry 'racism' over a councillor using the phrase 'Noo Joysey'.

Michael, Sheila and Molly remain. Painted large on Michael's barn are the words 'No more Trump lies. Michael has the respect and admiration of all the people who voted him Top Scot of the Year. Visiting his home, sitting in his living room (where there is a further wonderful painting of Forbes' former salmon fishing days by David McCue), having a coffee and petting his cats is a far more pleasurable, aesthetically pleasing, more natural, enjoyable experience than any round of Trump golf or stay at a Trump property, even the MacLeod House....

Trump has won a few battles here, but he will not get rid of this entrenched, formidable, honest opponent.

17: The Citizens Are Revolting -- But Not As Much As Trump Is

There may be corners of America where Trump is lauded as the second coming and people want to hear hate-filled speeches from the man cutting their healthcare and harming their industries, but he's not fooled many in the UK. Huge numbers of people in England, Ireland, Wales and Scotland are united in one thing: their hatred for the carrot-hued dictator.

He came to visit Theresa May and The Queen in July 2018. The response was overwhelmingly against him. There were rallies from Aberdeenshire to London, where a giant baby Trump blimp awaited him at Trafalgar Square.

Small section of anti-Trump rally, London, July 2018 (S Kelly)

True to form, May would not listen to the many calls to simply cancel the visit. After all, a woman hanging onto power by a fingernail who won't listen to six million petition signers is not going to be swayed by a sense of ethics or the wishes of people and dump Trump. She had Trump visit Windsor to see WWII veteran, Queen Elizabeth. Insiders said that the queen did subtle mischievous little things to signal her understandable disdain. Apparently, the level of hospitality Turnip and his First 'Lady' were of the lowest kind that protocol would allow, and the visit was visibly not of the same respectful, friendly reception given to President Obama. The queen is said to have worn a brooch to meet Trump which Obama had given her.

When asked whether the queen disliked Trump, our well-placed source did not directly answer. They replied with a question, asking: 'Do you suppose a woman who served in World War II fixing engines and rarely missed an engagement in decades of service would be pleased to welcome a man who evaded national service and spent time eating KFC and dodging security briefings?'

The baby blimp was wonderful; the creative protestors wanted to take it to Turnberry too – but were met with obstructions. Some in Turnberry cling to the idea of Trump as saviour and employer; with reverses at the historic property mounting, we will see how long that lasts.

The Trafalgar square protestors had great signs; one read 'Help me find his Horcruxes'. The baby Trump was put on a lion, and it was a peaceful afternoon.

For reasons best known to herself, Theresa May is having Trump return. For reasons best known to himself, he's accepted. The blimp is being readied. Those in the know are betting May will be ousted before such a visit happens again, but that may just be wishful thinking. Perhaps the 'forget human rights, racism, sexism and habitual lying – if I'm making money, nothing else matters' attitude sums up the pro-Trump Scot, few though they are.

18: A Degree Of Embarrassment – RGU Honours Degree Removed: Trump B*tchslapped

2010: Sir Ian Wood and Trump, resplendent in caps and gowns shared a glowing moment when Wood handed Trump an honorary degree from Robert Gordon University. Somehow, not everyone was as happy as the two billionaires.

Dr David Kennedy, a man who has dedicated his life to education, a former principal of RGU, handed back his own RGU degree in disgust. The moment made headlines and was captured in 'You've Been Trumped.' The university said the degree was for Trump's entrepreneurial achievements (presumably nothing to do with hiring illegal immigrants as cheap labour in the US, links to organised crime, bankruptcies and discouraging non-white people from buying his New York apartments). Kennedy on returning his degree said giving Trump an honour was: "quite preposterous."

Some of those who signed the petition, started by an Aberdeen Voice reporter, had some choice words for Trump and RGU.

As one signatory commented on the petition, there were: "Too many reasons to list." – David P. 3 years ago.

Other quotes included:

"This odious man thinks he can do as he likes in Scotland and bullies to get his own way" – Janet A. 3 years ago - *Game*

"What happened in Germany in the 1930's can happen anywhere. Trump demonising Muslims is every bit as odious as Hitler demonising Jews." – Alastair R. 3 years ago – *Set*

"RGU has to take a stance against this hateful bigot. His honorary degree soils all the genuine degrees and I am ashamed to be associated with this nasty, hateful dangerous man." – Paul D. 3 years ago – *Match*.

The petition is still online at the 38 Degrees website for anyone interested in further opinions held on Mr Trump's honour or (now) lack thereof.

Aberdeen Voice did contact Sarah Malone-Bates in her role as spokesperson for Trump at Menie, but for some reason, answer came there none. (In fact, Voice reporters have written to the spokeswoman at least ten times over the years with no response).

Will Sorial cover this chapter in his hotly-anticipated book of 11 June? If there is a lesson in here about winning, it will be an interesting one. Verdict: Trump was KO'd.

19: MacLeod House Debacle – Renaming and Tartan Tarting-up of a Once-Fine House – Loss

Here's how to convince Scotland not to love you: don't stop at insulting Scottish farmers or trying to stop sand dune systems from moving. Don't stop at comparing wind farms to the Lockerbie bombing. Seal the deal by taking a fairly historic property, stripping it of its historic name, and renaming it after your mum who lived hundreds of miles from it. Top it off by putting a cheesy concrete fountain in front of it. And fill it with your newly-commissioned Trump Tartan and Trump-crested furniture – all while insulting the neighbours and banning Glenfiddich. The Scots will be eating out of your hands. Or not.

Yes, people go there and have weddings; yes, it's popular in some circles. But certainly not everyone thinks this six-diamond resort is all that.

As to the American-Italian fountain, if a shortbread biscuit that looked like a willy upset the tender Mrs Bates, what must she think of this fountain with its naked cement putti's Mario carts? The poor lions with water gushing out of their jaws look embarrassed to be there. At the base of where some of these feline fountains sit – I kid you not – is a man making the trademark Trump 'OOO' mouth shape; this man has a full long head of hair.

Flagpole, fountain and MacLeod House by S Kelly

Inside the rooms, a duvet and orange pillows the colour of radioactive dyed cheddar cheese seem to dominate. Perhaps the tycoon when specifying the décor was trying to say he wanted it 'original' but 'orange' came out instead (the poor man could not pronounce this word in a speech in March 2019 any more than he could pronounce 'anonymous' -- or is that 'anomenoush?').

Delightful descriptions of how wonderful MacLeod House is can be found among other places... on the Press & Journal and Evening Express websites. Not everyone is equally impressed by the cheesy American Brigadoon remodelling and the venue:

One reviewer mentioned their cocktails arriving in plastic glasses and a 'disgusting' fig dessert, and said: "…we probably will go back, despite the service being poor, although staff were friendly...it's just not as good as I would have expected from a place of such reputation." - Kirsty

Many other Trip Advisor reviews are positive if not glowing. Some are not:

"Inside it is TRUMP all over and done to a very good standard (not the "paintings" which are truly cheap and awful). To be fair this hotel is not my personal taste but have to say if a mix of Versace and Liberace are your thing you will be in seventh heaven!

"We were in the bar being served drinks by the night porter and a late arriving party of 7 arrived, half way through our order the bartender actually disappeared to check in the guests and then carry their luggage to their rooms! Unbelievable!

"I am left sitting at the bar with half my order and my guests requesting a drink. Simply unacceptable in a cheap hotel but I am sure Mr T would have kittens if it happened to him!

The night porter apologised and in fairness this is not his fault as he was on his own but whoever manages and does the rota should allow for two staff in such an establishment?" – Richard S

Why, it's almost as if Trump just hired a pretty face who had no clue.

20: The War On Hate Speech – A win, a Mexican stand-off or a Trump Defeat? – Your Call

If the reader won't mind, the best way to tell this story seems to be in the first person. This section will also be a bit light on the satire front; satire is peppering this collection of works unevenly, but hopefully the rationale is clear. I don't want to get the bejeesus sued out of me.

I have a few Mexican relatives. They were in school when

Trump made his uncalled for, unhelpful remarks about Mexicans in the US illegally all being drug dealers and rapists. Even if I didn't know a single Mexican soul, this kind of hate in a would-be president was stirring me up. The hate speech against Mexicans spread from Trump's words about illegals to basically any Mexican in the USA. This spread quickly to schools, doing untold damage to children whether on the receiving end or the hate-filled end. Reports of prejudice and hate in the classroom reached the world. Does Mexico have organised crime and drug problems? Obviously. So does the USA. The people I knew from Mexico were keen students or people trying to legally remain in the US, working hard, and it was people like them getting abuse, not any criminals.

Trump already had form for insulting every race, nationality, religion, sexual persuasion and women. But he was never being considered for a governmental role, let alone the presidency before. I was at the time visiting Menie and writing about the things I saw there, from security guards badly treating the residents and stretching their remit past what I thought was legal through to mounds of rubbish, people concerned about wildlife and the environment. I was not happy.

I was going to Tripping Up Trump meetings too, and was impressed by all the dignified, legal, adult ways people were finding to combat Trump.

Slowly the idea of a petition started to form. I weighed the many cons which seemed to outweigh the potential pros. I put the idea on the backburner.

Then Trump mocked respected New York Times reporter Serge Kovaleski who has a debilitating condition impacting his joints. Trump did this as only a privileged, uncontrolled bully with arrested development could or would do – in my opinion. I wasn't just sick about it, I was infuriated, perhaps more scared as to what Trump would do if he got political power. Any doubts about whether to do the petition went away in the moment Trump waived his arms around and shook his head. Trump denies he mocked the man – a man with considerably more intellect than Trump will ever hope to achieve. If you watch the video, easily found on line, decide for yourself whether this is an act of mocking or not. If it is not mocking, what is it supposed to be? Trump makes bizarre hand and arm movements all the time, but never like that, and never while quoting someone.

I knew some people would ridicule the petition idea, and I didn't want to do it if TUT was against it. I told TUT what I planned, they seemed to like the idea, I went ahead. Within a week or so, the relevant petitions committee agreed wording for the petition with me, and off we went.

The way it seemed, I thought it would be a huge victory if it got any UK press or indeed any attention at all. I had intended it to be a stand against hate speech – which as I keep trying to tell people is different from free speech. I wanted to raise awareness; that's all. It seemed impossible that it would ever reach the ten thousand signature mark. By the time it closed, it reached 586,000 signatures.

I am still cross at what I consider to be patronising and sneaky behaviour from MP Mike Flynn. I had him on the phone around the time of the debate in his role as a petitions committee member, and as he put it, no one wanted to deal with the debate. "It 'landed on my desk' he said; and I seem to remember his mansplaining to me what the expression meant unbidden.

Before the debate I did an exhausting amount of press calls; I hadn't planned on so much interest. I'd be in my 9-5 job spending lunch times taping interviews or going live, and going to the BBC studio to do world service or other international interviews at night. I was filmed on location both at Menie, in Aberdeen, and in London by the statue of Boudicca and Parliament. I was talking on the World Service; it seems like only yesterday. Fitting it all in was fun. I did a live radio programme from the Altens Burger King ladies' room on my way to the BBC's studios after work

The night before the petition, while exhausted, I got one further call from the BBC – Flynn had put out a press statement that he was against my petition.

I didn't even quite take in the enormity of that pre-emptive strike until it was too late; I was so tired by then. I believe he had absolutely no business interfering with the desire of 586,000 people who wanted the matter fairly debated: you can't have a fair debate if the petitions committee member has come out against the outcome before the debate occurs. He won't comment on the subject to me these days – I'd tried various means to get an answer. I believe he blocked me on Twitter.

At any rate, I didn't think Trump would ever get banned, although that was what I wanted, what all the signatories wanted – and what should happen under UK law to people preaching hate – just as had been done to over 100 other hate preachers before.

I wonder where we'd be today had Trump's presidential bid – which could have been dealt a decisive blow by Parliament – flopped. Would we be letting this monster separate families and cage children – while he blames Obama? Would America be building a wall and taking bulldozers to butterflies and habitats while others starve? Would Steve Bannon be helping UK bigots organise?

However, on the day of the debate we got a spectacular show. Conservatives, Labour, all sorts of MPs queued up to denounce Trump and hate speech. Save for one or two individuals, notably the Turnberry MP who was so much in favour of the 'economic benefits' of Trump; she was outraged as I recall. I wonder if she still feels the same today? Trump was called a 'buffoon' by all sides; I can't recall seeing Parliament so very united before then. Several media organisations wanted me to go to London to comment; by then I felt the petition belonged as much to the signatories as it did to me. And quite frankly, I was knackered.

Trump's proposed Muslim America travel ban came just after my petition went live. If Trump hadn't mocked the reporter, then the Muslim travel ban would have been the catalyst for me instead. Some seven to eleven million Muslims were estimated to live in the US at the time of my petition; William Celli, the would-be bomber wanted to kill / injure as many as he could. He said Trump inspired him, as did two brothers in Boston who beat an Hispanic man with a pipe breaking his nose: 'Trump was right' they said about immigrants.

How anyone with access to news of Celli or these other gross instances of bullying and prejudice by Trump could have cast a vote for the man remains beyond me. I hope somewhere that some sociologists, psychiatric experts and exorcists are looking into it.

The Muslim ban seems to have got one or two of Trump's Middle East real estate deals cancelled. Perhaps attacking the main religion of a region where you want to do deals is not a gangbuster idea after all. There does seem to be some Saudi/ Trump bromance still in the air; I understand 'Little Adam Schitt' is looking into it. That could be yet another 'win' for the Oompa-Loompa in Chief.

Someone started a petition not to ban him or some such. It did fairly well, although there is a question as to where the signatories came from.

Heartbreakingly for me, two people I greatly admire were against my petition – Ian Hislop and J K Rowling. I maintain that prejudice and racism in the USA, a country steeped in anti-black sentiment from slavery days that never left huge swathes of the population, is a different animal than it is in the UK. It is partially fuelled by extremist, far right evangelicals and their at-home education, which for some is more of an indoctrination into the superiority of the white (pseudo) Christian male over every other race, sex and religion. Girls married off at 14 and 15 with no say are used to create more of these indoctrinated people – people with votes – people who love Trump. People who do what their religious leaders or their husbands tell them too. (Those wanting further information might visit UNICEF's page which discusses organisations such as 'Unchained at Last' which helps girls/women forced into marriage in the USA https://www.unicefusa.org/stories/front-lines-fight-end-child-marriage-us/35587).

There is ignorance and hate in the UK obviously; but there is a difference in terms of tolerance which I think in part has to do with education and the absence of colonial slavery here. I somehow have never been able to forget one of my visits to Florida while living in the UK. Not very far from Miami's cosmopolitan streets I'd wandered into a sports bar. Tiger Woods was taking a shot on a giant plasma screen. 'GET THAT N*GGER OFFA THAT TELEVISION!!' was shouted with amazing volume by a very unattractive, pale, slim older white man with red hair. Some of the clientele just laughed, most paid no attention. I had to leave. I have often spoken up against people making remarks like that. However, I was alone, there were dozens of them, and I was 90% certain they all had guns.

The UK is different – and having hate speech laws is, I think, one of the reasons why. Like every freedom, freedom of expression should have limits and it is not rocket science to weed out hate speech from exercising freedom of speech. If your speech is designed to hurt, inspire violence, or get others killed – it is illegal here but legal in the US, which allows the KKK to thrive. The KKK endorsed Trump as their presidential choice. He is, to me, their man through and through as apparently were some of his ancestors. Thoroughly disgusting. They are openly marching.

The USA needs gun control laws before more people are mown down; it also needs to address the boundaries that should exist on free speech.

For my troubles with the petition I got a large amount of praise and almost as much abuse. I would do it all again in an instant, even if a woman wrote to me that 'I was a traitor to Western civilisation' and if a man in the USA wrote to say I should never go back 'where we can get our hands on you' and that 'my fingers should be put to good use picking cotton instead of writing' – these types just love getting the slavery imagery going.

I learned a lot from the petition exercise. I saw that one person can have a positive effect, even if briefly, just as surely as the words of a president wanting to see journalists hurt contributed to four reporters being shot dead in Maryland. I consider this a 'win' if I have to use Trump speak. It was a positive experience to my way of thinking.

Trump was ridiculed in Parliament, over half a million people coming out against him, he lost business in the Middle East. It was all a bit crazy, but I'm glad I did it, and I'd do it again.

21: Hospitality PR Offensive – An Ongoing Series Of Blunders

I have no doubt Sarah Malone-Bates used all of her experience of event planning to make Trump International Golf Links Scotland the resounding, popular success it is today.

This should have been easy with the puff pieces her husband obligingly printed. Reviews of the delicious food, accounts of the wonderful MacLeod house surely would have had them queuing up to get in.

The five-star hotel which advertised Santa's Grotto is just what the jet-setter looks for when deciding where to stay. Between that and the Trump-crested furniture with the rich mold spore mustard fabric, how could you say no to the £295 per room per night package? The chef will even leave you a platter of food and a glass of champagne on arrival [but not a willie shaped shortbread]. You also get dinner and breakfast.

Perhaps we'll see you at the Vintage garden party where there will be a prize for the best dressed (will it be Sarah?). Maybe you'll attend the gin lamp making workshop [do what now? – Ed].

I'm sure the wealthy will abandon Grand Hotel du Cap Ferrat, Courcheval, Malibu and their other usual destinations to visit Trump on the cold, rainy Scottish east coast.

The TIGLS website's account of the history of the Trump maternal ancestors, the MacLeod family, who lived several hundred miles away at Stornoway, includes a line which may interest Trump mental health watchers:

"In terms of public health, the Rev John Cameron makes the following statement 'there is one peculiar distemper prevalent in this island, which seizes infants about the fifth night after their birth, and carries them off in convulsive fits'. The local surgeon believed that this was due to the excessive humidity of the region. This may be an explanation why so many Stornoway births in the 1855 registers do not give a forename. Perhaps the children died before they were baptized."

That Trump's superior gene pool is linked to inexplicable convulsive fits in infancy is personally something I might have left off the biog, but there you go.

Overall, the effect of all the parties, packages, Trump family history, etc on the website gives you a warm glow and a deep insight into the history of this colourful president, and I'm certain American tourists will flock to the place – any day now.

David Milne, who lives in the former coastguard station overlooking the parking lot reports over the years that the parking lot is rarely crowded. Only a snob – or public relations professional – would conclude there is an air of desperation and a whiff of 'please come and spend money here' about the website. But admit it – the package with the 'glass of fizz' on arrival and the use of the outdoor hot tub is tempting.

In what other ways is the Trump PR battles being won? There's ingratiating himself with the neighbours by covertly trying to buy their homes on the cheap, insulting them, and Donald saying on film to Sarah that wants to tear David Milne's home down - and Sarah agreeing to it, as captured in Anthony Baxter's first movie. There's the reactionary, back-footed constant issue of defiant, aggressive, denial-drenched statements from 'a Trump spokeswoman' every time a negative Trump fact comes out (and that's quite often it must be said). There's throwing the opening party which BrewDog attended to sell beer –not long after which the company issued 'Mr President' beer. The label reads in part "This is a Defcon 1 of IPA's. An all out bedrock patriot, hell-bent on global domination"

The PR war is also fought by giving money to local charities – some of which don't want to be associated with the organisation, some of which stick steadfast to their patron. Then there's the battle to plaster the Trump logo on as many websites, press releases and even school children's sports kits as possible.

Alas. The losses on the PR front are mounting. It's surprising how what works for a benign countryside museum doesn't necessarily translate to an international 'Six Diamond' resort owned by a tax-cheating bigot – sorry – I mean owned by an athletic, big-brained president.

22: The Milne border skirmish – a loss

What is it with building borders and bunds? Not content with having minions plant border flags in a field Michael Forbes has used for years with no warning, Trump turned his eye on the cottage he wanted ripped down, and decided to do some 'winning'

David and his wife Moira live in the former coastguard lookout station sitting on a hill overlooking the parking lot, clubhouse and Susan Munro's property. Before you could say 'Trump must stick to the approved plan', Trump had thrown up bunds of sandy dirt by the boundary of Milne's land and by Susan Munro's cottage. The TIGLS people kept planting fir trees on top of these bunds – banks of steep sandy earth coming to a fairly narrow top – I should know, a German film crew had me walk on top of one. There is a reason we don't usually see forests of conifer trees growing in sandy soil near the beach – they can't. Still, TIGLS keeps planting these poor things – or at least he did for several years once the bunds were up – and as they inevitably died, he just bought more. There seems something childish, brutish and immoral about continuously planting trees that don't have a chance to live, doesn't there? In his witty stoic way Milne isn't bothered, and said he thanks the Trump team for all the useful firewood they're providing.

Then Trump decided that part of Milne's garage – in situ for decades – was on Trump land by a few inches. Little more has come of this – but the bluster of the attack was quite possibly to worry the Milne family.

One day the family returned home and found an ugly, high,

cheap wood and wire fence had been put up on a border of their land- and arguably on their land. In the process some of the Milne's possessions were broken.

As the New York Times summed up the situation: "David and Moira Milne had already been threatened with legal action by Mr. Trump's lawyers, who claimed that a corner of their garage belonged to him, when they came home from work one day to find his staff building a fence around their garden. Two rows of grown trees went up next, blocking the view. Their water and electricity lines were temporarily cut. And then a bill for about $3,500 arrived in the mail, which, Mr. Milne said, went straight into the trash."

Milne also foretold in the Times' 2016 article that Mexico would not be paying for any wall, either. Perhaps George and Donald are proud of their border wall win? Trump has just used his presidential veto to overturn the House on the matter. Let's hope there is an impeachment before any further environmental and human casualties occur at the Mexican border. I don't understand where the United Nations is; aside from the jailing of families of asylum seekers, separating them from their children, the deaths in custody of some of these unfortunates, the 'missing' ones adopted by American families, a woman has just been told she will not get her child back from its adoptive parents. Anyone supporting this policy and this president might want to do some soul searching, particularly if they think god is behind Trump. But I digress again.

The Milnes' home is a delightful place, the ugly fencing and trees Donald plants cannot change that, and the Milnes will not be moved. A Mexican flag as well as the Scottish Saltire proudly fly over the former coastguard station: and no, they don't need to have a giant flagpole or oversized flags.

David Milne has written two books so far on the Trump invasion of Menie, 'Blinded by the Bling' and 'It's only Sand!' They are yugely recommended, and why he was asked to consider publishing this work. Yes, Milhouse is my publisher too; I selected them, and was glad they accepted me.

23: The Global Scot Debacle – Sturgeon Trumps Drumpf

Oops! George didn't see this one coming – Nicola Sturgeon revoked Trump's 'Global Scot' status. In other words, she doesn't want him to be in any form an ambassador for Scotland in the wider world – wherever his mother was born or however much fake tartan and family crests he's ordered.

Not long after Trump lost his RGU honorary degree, Sturgeon made her move with little warning.

First Minister Jack McConnell gave Drumpf this honorary business ambassadorship in 2006.

You can sort of see why Nichola axed Trump if you look at this description of who a Global Scot is:

"Global Scots are experienced professionals who have built their reputations in the highest echelons of the international marketplace and they have a real desire to give something back by helping Scottish companies to develop and grow. Since 2001, they have contributed significantly to Scotland's economic growth."

In other words, being a racist or accessing beauty contestant's changing rooms doesn't fit.

The bellowing billionaire, haemorrhaging money from his Scottish ventures has hardly contributed significantly to Scotland's economic growth. He has built a reputation not least from his over 3,000 lawsuits and locking immigrant children in cages, but what may be a win to the unholy trio involved in his forthcoming biog, it's just not necessarily a reputation that reflects that well on Scotland.

The FT reported on the loss of the title, coming as it did on the heels of RGU taking back its honorary degree, saying:

"Mr Trump's recent remarks have shown he is no longer fit to be a business ambassador for Scotland, according to a government spokesperson…"

Those remarks included his call for a 'total and complete [if something is total, isn't it complete?] shutdown' on Muslims travelling to the US (forgetting the States has a Muslim population).

Poor Donald; where would he find an outlet to express his reaction to this yuge loss of face? Surprisingly (or not), his reaction found a home at The Aberdeen Press & Journal.

For some reason, no reporter's name is given to the P&J piece in which Donald issues these prophetic words:

"I only said what needed to be said [in his 'ban Muslims' speech, which conveniently made no mention of white male terrorism, which is mowing people of all ages down in America, rising since his election], and when I am elected no one will be tougher or smarter than me. I will work very hard and effectively to defeat terrorism. [no president has done more to increase the wealth of golf resorts, we concede, but as to defeating terrorism, would-be terrorists are increasingly linked to Trump and his hate-filled speeches and rallies. We are two minutes to midnight on the doomsday clock because of this presidency].

"The UK politicians should be thanking me instead of pandering to political correctness." Trump concluded per the P&J.

This example of equating political correctness to not being a hateful xenophobe is something that may work on double-digit IQ undereducated Americans from homogenous communities who go to Trump rallies, but it does not wash here.

Perhaps we should all pause to remind ourselves how grateful we should be?

24: The world's largest dune system claim – a monumental cock-up by TIGLS

Sue Kelly
@SueKelly10

@realDonaldTrump Fake news? why sign erectd at ur Menie club-world's largest dunes not there dude. (hear ur happy 2 have any kind of erectn)

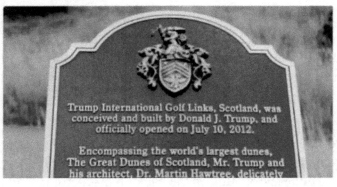

Trump International Golf Links, Scotland, was conceived and built by Donald J. Trump, and officially opened on July 10, 2012.

Encompassing the world's largest dunes, The Great Dunes of Scotland, Mr. Trump and his architect, Dr. Martin Hawtree, delicately

Not far from the Trump Golf Clubhouse at the Trump Golf Course stands this Trump plaque which reads:

"Trump international Golf Links, Scotland, was conceived and built by Donald J. Trump, and officially opened on July 10, 2012. Encompassing the world's largest dunes [sic], The Great Dunes of Scotland [wtf?], Mr Trump and his architect. Dr. Martin Hawtree, delicately weaved [very sic] these magnificent golf holes through this unparalleled 600 acre site running along the majestic North Sea. The unprecedented end result is, according to many, the greatest golf course anywhere in the world!"

It is only 76 words, and yet it tells us so much about the man. Seventy-six words – and no one – not a soul from the writer of these delicately-written lines through the firm that created this plaque – stepped up to the plate and said 'this is wrong'.

Architect Dr Martin Hawtree* will be thrilled to be memorialised as the creator of the links in the world's largest sand dune system. I can practically picture him and Donald now, riding camels, stopping at the occasional oasis and eating figs while on their journey through these massive dunes. The conceiving sounds rather painful. The delicacy involved leaves one speechless.

Not everyone is expected to know which are the world's largest sand dunes which are popularly thought to be in Namibia. However, any school child could reasonably be expected to guess that they wouldn't be on the shore of a fairly small country like Scotland.

Despite having the big fat brain Trump continually tells us he has due to his superior genes, no doubt the world's largest genes, he either wrote this on the back of an Aderol packet and demanded the plaque be created, or he approved of it (who at TIGLS would dare create such a thing on their own initiative?). The Great Dunes of Scotland do not exist, save in the mind of one Donald J Trump. Not even the presence of the distinctive, tasteful Trump family crest can save this plaque.

No one would create such a monstrous monument to ignorance without Trump's instructions. There are only a few possibilities: the people who saw this wording as it passed from idea to finished product (NB I feel better about my prose already) either: a. were too afraid to correct the error, b. were too uneducated to know there was a problem, c. didn't care what this would do to the Trump reputation in the eyes of the visitors, or d. wanted the orange tycoon to be a laughing stock. I rather hope Option D played a part somewhere along the line, perhaps at the foundry. Options A and or B may well have been relevant to Mrs Bates. I suspect we will never know.

Anti-Trump activists still drop by to have their photo taken with this plaque. The golfers who have just paid heavily for their round of golf and exit the clubhouse (where coffee and sandwiches for 4 can run to about £80 it is said) are no doubt delighted that so very much attention to detail has been applied.

What Freud would have made of Trump's preoccupation with size – everything seems to need to be biggest with him, not least the giant flagpole at Menie and the one in Florida. In Florida a multi-million-dollar suit was brought by Trump over his desire to have a flagpole far higher than planning permission allowed; he claimed that his 'human rights' were being infringed, poor soul. Killjoy Florida planning personnel claimed they didn't want the thing being a hazard to navigation.

* For some reason there are people with doctorates involved in planning in Aberdeen city and shire, and with this course, who seem hell bent on being addressed as 'Dr', which may be accurate but is none the less pompous for it. The doctor behind many of Aberdeen's ancient buildings being surrounded by cheap glass and steel curtain walls and the skyline losing all sense of coherence is one Dr Maggie Bochel, now departed to the private sector. At a public hearing to determine whether a football stadium would be built on land that previous generations had decided would never be built on because of its beauty and importance to wildlife, she was addressed as Mrs Bochel by a councillor 'Dr Bochel' Maggie corrected.

25: You can't fight Mother Nature – Trump humiliated

SK: "Hello I'd like to speak to Professor Ritchie please?"

(muffled voice in background)

"who's calling?"

SK: "Suzanne Kelly"

Muffled voice in background "I'm not home"

"He's not home."

And so went the last call I placed to Professor Bill Ritchie. He and I were once on the 'East Grampian Coastal Partnership' project together when I was a community councillor. The idea was to take the Torry, Aberdeen area and improve its amenities for the public including an educational element and environmental conservation. It never happened, and I haven't been able to find out concrete reasons why the plan was scuppered. Instead, there will be an incinerator, and the Bay of Nigg, which had two SSSI designations and which the public used to freely enjoy, will now be a commercial harbour, fenced off to the public. The SSSI designation in Scotland is now toast. They say the project is to entice cruise ships; smart money is on industrial usage including breaking of decommissioned oil platforms. There goes the air quality. I didn't have asthma until I moved to the area. It turns out that particulate pollution in this area was off the charts and had been above EU safe levels for ages. This mysteriously changed with no remedial action being taken, coincidentally just before the harbour expansion project got the go-ahead.

I next heard of Bill Ritchie when he popped up on the Scottish Reporter's report approving Trump's plans. Ritchie said in effect there was no reason Trump and nature couldn't co-exist, and he was made chairman of the Menie Environmental Monitoring Advisory Group (MEMAG).

Absolute Rubbish – mixed waste on Trump land March 2013

Aberdeen Voice got wind of burrowing animals being gassed-as is done on golf courses. Then we got wind of a mountain of mixed rubbish. With the help of a Tripping Up Trump member, we got photos of this amazing rubbish, heaped in two piles on the estate. A complaint was made to SEPA. We understand one of the few outcomes was that a local farmer with nothing resembling the rubbish tips getting cautioned.

But on MEMAG ran, under the good professor's stewardship. Only Trump MEMAG members didn't attend meetings. Requested data was not forthcoming. Then one day, the whole thing just fizzled out.

In June 2010 Aberdeenshire Council papers read:

"An Environmental Management Plan (EMP) has been submitted for the Championship Golf Course. The plan covers the construction, establishment and operational phases of the championship golf course. The plan has a ten-year lifespan to cover the three main development phases of the course. The document contains a summary of other management plans and should be read in conjunction with the Habitat Management Plan. The plan has been formulated to reconcile the constructional and operational measures required to fulfil the design brief of a functional high-quality Championship Golf Course and the necessary constraints imposed by the sensitive nature of the development site"

Not for lack of trying, but the good professor, the council and Scottish government agencies are rather quiet in response to questions on how this ten-year lifespan / coverage for three development phases was allowed to simply die off.

George A Sorial, chronicler of Trump's wins in Scotland is quoted in the Herald on the matter:

"Having successfully completed its scrutiny role for the construction of the championship golf course, MEMAG was dissolved," said George Sorial, executive vice-president and counsel for the Trump organisation in New York.

"Sorial insisted that the golf links had not done much harm to the Site of Special Scientific Interest (SSSI) it was built on. "More than 95 per cent of the SSSI remains untouched and the ecological diversity of the site remains intact," he said.

Well, when a member of a Team Trump gives you a figure, that's good enough for me. Chemicals sprayed, burrowing animals presumably despatched, food sources for animals stripped away to make greens and paths – and the ecological diversity of the site remains intact. And all this with 95 percent of the

SSSI untouched. (notice how often figures quoted by Trump personnel are so often in the 90s by the way – Trump's 93% approval rating, his promise the federal government will pay 90% of Florida hurricane recovery costs, etc...) Sorial found no time to explain what happened to the ten-year monitoring and the fact MEMAG was to cover three projects. But why split hairs over the UK's only moving sand dune system?

As previously mentioned, the Ferret covered the disappearance of MEMAG too, with a quote from First Minister Nicola Sturgeon:

"Scotland's First Minister warned the US President Elect that he had to abide by the law like everyone else. "Nobody can escape the environmental responsibilities that the law imposes on them and that's true of Donald Trump as it is of any other business owner..."

Perhaps we need the First Minister to take a peek at the current state of play before any cheap, fugly – sorry, beautiful, luxury houses go up?

The Ferret continued:

"Trump's representatives, however, often failed to turn up for meetings. According to the minutes of MEMAG meetings shared by Aberdeen Voice, his Scottish spokeswoman, Sarah Malone, gave her apologies to meetings in April 2011 and May 2012.

At the May 2012 meeting MEMAG described the Trump organisation's failure to attend recent meetings as "unfortunate". It agreed to write to the organisation "noting the need for representation at MEMAG meetings..."

Not only did the meetings end because Sarah was too busy, but for some funny reason, all of the minutes had disappeared from public view. Happily, Aberdeen Voice had saved oh, let's say 95 per cent of these, which it happily shared with the Ferret, and which can now be found on line for posterity. (No need to thank us Sarah or Professor Ritchie).

Going back into the first person again momentarily, I wish to extend the thanks that are due to the good professor for his testimony on Trump's behalf to the Reporters which helped no doubt secure planning permission, and for his keen, brilliant management of MEMAG. Trump could not have done it without him.

As to SNH and the shire, no doubt they are as keen to put wildlife before money as they always have been.

These photos illustrate my own amateur environmental monitoring. Well, someone has to do it. Other members of Tripping up Trump frequently visit the course and report back to the group on what's going on; one woman seems tireless in keeping an eye on the estate and the coast and has done a lot of important work. Reports of Sarah Malone putting out bird seed and suet balls are however, thin on the ground.

Now that's what you call caring for the environment - detail of rubbish tip at Menie

March 2013 (S Kelly)

A pretence at attractiveness but in reality, a dyed, unkempt unhealthy mess held together with sprays; a recurring Trump theme, February 2013 (S Kelly)

(This one is considerably clearer in colour, available in the ebook version via Amazon)

Could all of this been avoided if Trump's parents had just let him have a sandbox? - Near the collapsed Blairton Burn February 13 (S Kelly)

This is how you manage the UK's only moving sand dune system. This is how Aberdeenshire Council and SEPA enforce environmental monitoring. This is how TIGLS cooperates with Professor Ritchie to monitor the environment. This is the record planning and councillors base their approval on. They might all be patting themselves on the back on this yuge 'win'.

However, if they think they've won hearts and minds, perhaps their usual cockiness is misplaced.

26: A government coup: How a petition for Truth became a whitewash

The way David Milne's petition to Holyrood for an investigation into what happened at Menie AFTER Trump got his planning permission leaves a stain on every organisation that turned it into a whitewash.

David is a patient, quiet man who, with his wife Moira, have been through quite enough because of Trump. From the threats to tear his home down to the building of a fence and attempt to get the Milnes to pay, they have weathered storms.

David's books 'Blinded by the Bling' and 'It's only Sand!' should be on the reading list of every follower of this incredible saga. He is a walking compendium of facts about Trump, planning, government.

His petition was launched on 14 February 2013 and swiftly drew 19,400 signatories. Mr Milne wanted, per the documents filed:

"I wish to see an inquiry to establish what communications and commitments were made in private to the Trump Organisation, and to consider whether there are improvements that can be made to procedure and best practice in the light of those findings, especially with regard to contact with planning applicants, the ability of Ministers to call in applications after rejection rather than allowing an appeal, and around equality of access to the planning process for both applicants and objectors."

What he and the public got was a whitewash: each involved government agency – Scottish Enterprise, Grampian Police (now subsumed in Police Scotland), Aberdeenshire Council, etc – was allowed to conduct its own self-investigation and issue its own letter to Holyrood. They all cleared themselves, proclaiming its innocence of any wrongdoing – without any scrutiny or independent investigation. Most of these took a narrow focus, different to the petition's remit of what happened after the permission was granted. How Mr Milne stayed composed during the Holyrood Petition Committee's sham of a hearing is a mystery.

In a BBC article, a Trump spokesperson is referred to as male; would it have been Sorial? A Trump son? Trump himself?

"The project has already gone through years of scrutiny and debate during a lengthy planning process, including a public inquiry in the full media spotlight.

"Mr Milne needs to move on. He attempted this before and it failed because there is no basis for it.

"The championship course is now established and drawing thousands of golfers from around the world and creating business opportunities and much needed jobs. [really?]"

"The second course would be named The Mary MacLeod Course, after Mr Trump's Scottish-born mother [because naming a course after your mum's going to endear you to the people whose coastline you're ruining].

"The unprecedented demand to play our championship course has accelerated our plans."

It does kind of matter who said this: if it was a Trump son exaggerating; quite possibly lyingthe demand has hardly accelerated plans; it has not been thousands as far as Tripping

Up Trump or those who could see the parking lot deduced), that is to be expected. In fact, it's genetic. If it is a lawyer, supposedly on some kind of ethics oath and responsible to a bar somewhere, exaggerating like this rather than spoilt brats fond of killing things, perhaps statements he's made elsewhere to other bodies need to be looked at. And if it were a lawyer: is it the one who wants you to buy his book about how great the winning is – and how much exaggeration will the pages hold?

The Petitions Committee were also very fond of redacting information. An Aberdeen Voice Reporter followed the proceedings at the time closely, and got this response to an email questioning the methodology, redaction, behaviour of the committee:

"In relation to procedure, the Scottish Parliament's public petitions process provides that the Public Petitions Committee shall take such action as it considers appropriate in relation to any petition and that it may close a petition at any time. There is no appeal process against a decision of the Committee."

– David Stewart MSP – email to me from Committee on Mon, 16 Sep 2013 16:12

Lots of people got coy about Jack Swinney's involvement with the Trump camp, which makes the Bromance between Donald and Alex in the early days seem coy. The information being redacted was, in some cases, information that had already been revealed by FOI requests (placed by an Aberdeen Voice reporter).

Here are extracts from a letter Jack Perry sent the Donald, from Aberdeen Voice' unredacted copy.

"You may or may not recall that I had the pleasure in October 2006 of joining you for lunch in the Trump Tower with the then First Minister, Mr Jack McConnell [SK says: 'tug that forelock' – the implication is that a man as busy/rich/famous

133

as Trump would not remember this poor wee Scottish civil servant – who was being used to grease wheels. 'Course Trump remembered him]. At that time, you shared with us your vision for the development for the Menie Estate. We at Scottish Enterprise (S) certainly shared your excitement over this project [how lovely!]. As the project developed, we believed and still do that the economic benefits to Scotland of this project were substantial. [Scottish Enterprise gets hundreds of millions per year – and aside from its several scandals, did they really believe building a further Scottish golf course while other courses were closing was good business sense?]

"Accordingly, we were profoundly dismayed by the decision made by the Aberdeenshire Council Infrastructure Committee to reject the planning application for this project. I recorded that disappointment in a personal letter to Ms Anne Robertson, Leader of Aberdeenshire Council. As you know, since then the Scottish Government has decided to 'call in' the application... [so is he implying that his letter – his personal letter – helped push the course forward? Is quango SE using taxpayer millions so unelected people can help billionaires ruin an SSSI site? You could think so]

"I have taken the liberty of discussing the matter with the Chairman of the Scottish Parliament's Enterprise, Energy and Tourism Committee to make him aware of our support for the project and to offer any evidence to him and his committee should they require [sic].

I have also now spoken about this matter to the Shadow Enterprise Ministers from the Labour and Liberal Democrat parties in the Scottish Parliament. I have tried to make it clear in these discussions that the impact of Aberdeenshire Council's decision goes far beyond the immediate issue of the Trump development but has much wider implications for Scotland's international image and reputation as a country which welcomes investment.

I have been greatly encouraged by the unequivocal support from the Scottish business community which your project was [sic] attracted [Sir Ian Wood, just to mention in passing, has strong links with SE and business communities. Just saying].… We shall continue to provide whatever evidence and support we can, should we be called to do so.

"For your information, I have also been greatly encouraged over the past few days by the support shown by the Aberdeen City and Shire Economic Forum [ACSEF] whose chairman, Mr Patrick Machray, has been very public and very vocal in support of the Trump development. Patrick is also the Chairman of Scottish Enterprise Grampian. As Scotland's principal economic development agency, we at Scottish Enterprise wish to see your development proceed. We will continue to do what we can to help.

CC (redacted), Lorna Jack, Patrick Machray"
– Perry to Trump 7 December 2007, sent via email to S Kelly Wed, 29 May 2013 16:17

Mr Milne vs Mr Millionaire was never going to end in David's favour.

Mr Milne said: "Now that I have finally finished laughing at the self-incriminating actions of the public petitions committee, I have to say I am saddened by their lack of interest in the facts of the matter. They have in effect proven my case better than I ever could have done, the way they so readily brushed aside facts that have been in the public domain for many years and have now given the appearance of trying to airbrush them out of existence, proves the need for an inquiry.

"They have shown that the governance of this country cannot be trusted and if they truly believe that the people of this country will quietly turn and walk away cowed and defeated, they are sadly mistaken"

An Aberdeen Voice article on the hearing can be found at Appendix II.

27: TIGLS' bid to spread its logo – beaten back (with a little AV help)

What is it about these big dictators wanting to see their logo smeared all over the place? Is there anything Trump owns that doesn't have his name or his logo on it (save Melania – we've seen her naked, and doesn't seem to have a Trump tattoo)?

Brand visibility, corporate branding – it seemed TIGLS was waging a battle to plaster the Trump logo on as many Scottish websites, press releases and even school children's sports kits as possible. They tried. They were beaten back.

For a little while the Trump logo could be found on public/ private scheme websites and some school children's football tops. Aberdeen Voice and Rob Edwards of the Ferret covered the football strip story, and the fact that Trump was allowed to use school children to plant grass on the moving sand dune system to stabilise it. Straight answers from the council are still awaited.

With regard to the sports kit, picture a smiling Sarah 'Face of Aberdeen' Malone posing inside a school with young footballers (and a few suits – who they are would be good to know). She holds the shoulders of a shirt, while a footballer holds the bottom; the shirt stretched for all to see the words 'Trump International Scotland' spelled out. The rest of the team, resplendent in Trump football jerseys are lined up in the background; the setting is a school. Nothing about the incident remotely smacks of Hitler Youth.

Aberdeen Voice's Freedom of Information requests to Aberdeenshire Council, which is only supposed to use private firms' logos in very limited circumstances, got the usual avoidance.

The council replied it was nothing at all to do with them, just with the 'The Balmedie Football club' which it said was run by a parent group as a separate entity within the Balmedie community. Although it is acknowledged that the majority of the children that played with that team will have been pupils at Balmedie School.

However, when Edwards wrote about the story – and this has just been realised fully in research for this book – he quoted a council spokesperson as saying the Trump sponsorship on the shirts was within their policy. Edwards' article reads:

"Aberdeenshire Council, however, insisted that the funding of the football kits was in line with the council's guidance. "A number of schools across Aberdeenshire have developed links with the businesses and facilities in their communities, and these are all brought forward with the best interests of pupils in mind." Said a council spokesman,

"It would be a shame to deny the pupils at Balmedie similar opportunities on this occasion simply because of media interest in the developer."

Yes, how could anyone deprive the otherwise shirtless nippers of the 'opportunity' of being able to display 'Trump International' on their kits as they played other area schools? By this time, it was obvious to everyone that Trump was linked to discrimination, anti-Muslim hate speech, and of course sexism.

So, which was it: Did Trump get permission from the council to put his name and logo on the shirts, or was it a private football club? Amazingly, Aberdeenshire Council has contradicted itself and appeared not to have followed rules on sponsorship or guidance on photographing children.

Aberdeenshire Council has been served a follow up to Aberdeen Voice's original FOI request, and we greatly anticipate how they will talk their way out of this one.

The photograph of the fragrant Mrs Bates with the footballers in Trump-crested kit seems to have been taken inside of an Aberdeenshire school: the council has also been asked to explain how permission was granted for the publicity photo and that the minors' parents consented. This should be, as they say, interesting.

As happy as the council were for this sponsorship – according to one council source anyway – and clearly allowed this photo to be taken – the council was furious when Councillor Martin Ford used council premises to talk to reporters on council business. As we say in New York, 'Go Figure.'

NB – 'Balmedie Football Club' do not seem to have a social media presence.

Before leaving the subject of children, there is a further disagreement about Trump's use of them and what the council should have done. Balmedie school children were used to plant marram grass on the once-moving sand dune systems to the dismay of many ecologists. The children planting the grass was also turned into a photo opp. The grass is used to stabilise the once moving sand dune system. You know, part of the environment Sorial said was 95% intact.

Turning back to Rob Edwards' article, Trump says it had Aberdeenshire's blessings for this exploitation; the eco schools people say otherwise;

"Balmedie is a designated 'eco-school' and Aberdeenshire Council claimed the eco-schools governing body was 'very supportive' of the planting. But this was dismissed as 'incorrect' by Keep Scotland Beautiful (KSB), which oversees eco-schools.

"We were not aware of the involvement of the Trump Organisation," a KSB spokeswoman told the Sunday Herald. "It's not something that we would support, endorse or be consulted on."

Perhaps the reason they would not have been consulted is that they would not have endorsed or supported moves to stabilise the UK's only moving sand dune system and its wildlife. Believe it or not, the Trump spokeswoman would not comment on the matter.

Aberdeen Sports Village was approached by Aberdeen Voice. A copy of one of Trump's racist rants was sent with a request to drop the logo from the Sports Village's website saying the taxpayer and the Village should not be associated with racism. Without much fuss, the sign of the beast was taken off the site.

Another charity has declined to cease its links with Trump, clinging onto his money. Pointing out his racism and his cuts to Obamacare, otherwise known as the Affordable Care Act, were costing lives, the charity in question dismissed the approach as being 'political.' If it's political to be against people dying because they can't afford healthcare (which is eye-wateringly expensive in the USA) or because they oppose racism, perhaps being 'political' is not as sinful as the charity sniffily makes it sound.

Logos aside: the biggest scoop for any newspaper this century was also Trump's hugest, or should I say yugest, coup was the

EXCLUSIVE column Damian Bates gave Trump in the Press & Journal. If you missed your chance to appreciate Donald J Trump's massive column, you will be relieved to learn back issues of the paper can be purchased. Don't be the only one on your street not to have a framed copy of the column on your living room wall.

Words cannot fully express the admiration people experienced when Donald whipped out his great column for all to admire.

It brings a tear to the eye to realise that what The Donald did at Menie was his way of paying Scotland back.

What did we ever do to deserve it?

In the interests of both not using too much P&J material and not making readers ill, here are a few of Trump's moving words from April 2016. They may stir your heart. Try antacids.

"When I first arrived on the scene in Aberdeen, the people of Scotland were testing me to see just how serious I was – just like the citizens in the United States have done about my race for the White House.

I had to win them over – I had to convince them that I meant business and that I had their best interests in mind.

Well, Scotland has already been won – and so will the United States.

I saw the tide turn in Aberdeen when it became apparent that I was doing extensive research on environmental concerns and had hired the leading authorities on everything concerning this amazing land.

We worked with Scottish National Heritage and forged a partnership based on our collective interests. [I long suspected some kind of forging was going on; I also used to think that the

140

SNH was supposed to be objective]

Any mistrust was replaced by confidence in my ability as well as my dedication. [great fact-checking by Damian Bates' people here]

It honours my mother and has helped the economy of Scotland. My family and I are grateful to both Scotland and United States, and it feels good to give back."

If nothing else, Trump's words confirmed the suspicions many harboured about Scottish Natural Heritage – or Shootin N Huntin as it is un-affectionately known. Some sources claim Salmond told the SNH to fall in line with Trump. Whether or not that is true, it seems that they did. They allowed the SSSI environmental protection to be swept away for Trump-crested furniture, golf buggies, a giant flagpole, and a course subject to crumbling in bad weather.

Any Scottish quango or government branch that looked at Trump's past promises for his similar enterprises could have wondered whether his bluster was simply empty words and hot air. Failing to do so, failing to analyse the funding for the project has got us where we are today – a moving sand dune system wrecked, environmental havoc, chemicals, gassed burrowing animals, a fraction of promised jobs realised, a parking lot that is more empty than full, and no millions rolling into the local economy. Thanks all.

Mistrust misplaced? Tide turned in Aberdeen? Scotland won over? Was this before or after they sacked a chef for the contents of his Facebook page (someone at TIGLS seems to like going onto Facebook and seeking incriminating screenshots), or after the huge orange diapered baby Trump blimp was flown over Trafalgar Square by cheering thousands? We should be told.

28: Right To Roam – An Ongoing Fight

Any foreign investor in Scottish property with a decent lawyer would have discovered early on in any purchase negotiations that there is a right in Scotland to roam over public and private land.

With Sorial's help (and apparently the Russian's help too) Trump bought Menie, knowing people could come and go at all times, cross the course and walk wherever the code allowed them. Being such a people person, Trump probably relished the prospect of chance encounters with others.

Law in Scotland could not be plainer: citizens, visitors have a right to roam the countryside as long as they obey certain rules. Land owners are not to keep any gates permanently locked or hamper access.

Dozens of emails have been sent over the course of years to Aberdeenshire Council and other government agencies who are meant to enforce this law. When it comes to Trump, their efforts have been all but non-existent. Trump has, according to frequent visitors, planted gorse and other species that will spread across trails and make access for ramblers difficult to impossible. Trump does seem to be winning this war in terms of keeping the less able-bodied off his land, aided by his allies in Aberdeenshire planning.

The gate TIGLS put between its parking and Leyton Farm Road; locked shut. Walkers are forced to squeeze by either side of it – if they are fit and thin enough to do so. Aberdeenshire Council and its right to roam officers have been aware of this situation for years (S Kelly)

It is beyond dispute that this gate, erected at the end of Leyton Farm Road and the newly-built parking lot, serves no purpose but to keep people out. It is permanently locked shut; the lock seems to have rusted closed when last examined. No fire truck, no police car, no ambulance will enter that way. Should hundreds of homes ever get built, which many think will only happen after Trump sells up, what this will mean for emergency services access is a matter for concern. Mounds of earth either side of the incongruous gate, stuck where no gate was needed are planted with conifers making it impossible for anyone who's not slim or fairly fit to go around. When Aberdeen Voice visited in April 2019, one side of this gate had become completely impassable. Let's put it this way, the Donald is not expected to be seen any time in the near future shuggling his way around this entrance.

If the idea was to further block Susan Munro's family in their house, it does make a difference. If the idea is to further cut her views across what was once unspoilt lands to the sea, it again interferes with her enjoyment of her property.

Leyton Farm Road during the early construction period (when the gate was occasionally open) Photo by Rob Scot

During the construction phase of the clubhouse parking, the road became rutted extremely deeply. Funnily enough the Press & Journal had no room for such as story, although Aberdeen Voice did, which may have contributed to the resurfacing which took place not long after the article was out.

There are a number of emails back and forth with the council's right to roam enforcement boffins and Aberdeen Voice. The people meant to enforce this right have lots of words, but say little, and have enforced nothing. Trump may be getting away with hindering people, but he has not stopped everyone just yet. Verdict: no winners in that battle.

III World Wars

Trump and Sorial engaged in their brand of warfare and

winning all around the world (sorry if there are any flat-earthers readers). Here are some of their other campaigns. If George and Donald call this winning, who are we to argue?

New York

<u>Jones Beach</u>

Imagine what was until the 1980s a wholly unspoilt, long, sandy stretch of New York coastline filled with both bathers and wildlife. Then hospital waste started washing ashore where the horseshoe crabs lived. Some blamed the NY organised crime syndicates. Then something else foul showed up.

Donald Trump, for reasons that need some examination, somehow got a foothold in Jones Beach. Plans included taking over a section of the boardwalk and a beautiful, publicly-owned 1930s building. This is not invention: his plan involved digging several basement levels under the building into... the beach below the building.

His plans were eventually derailed thanks in part to an activist (one person can help turn the tide), litigation, concerns over flooding, and a large stormy disaster (Sandy, not Daniels).

Here we have a beautiful beach, open to all and home to nature, then Trump arrived and pulled some of the usual tricks from his playbook. Does any of this sound familiar?:

He

- bragged that thousands of jobs would be created: "It's not a big deal for me, but it's a deal that will produce 1,000 construction jobs and at least 500 jobs permanent, all the time," Trump said at a rally to try to push the project forward.

- paid protestors: "Trump was flanked by supporters he

bused in for the rally. Friedman spoke to some of them and says they were paid to appear." according to NPR.

- initially said he'd build a $40 million-pound luxury project – then wanted to scale it down to $24 million.

- initially started work – then did virtually nothing for ages. As local media News 12 put it: "Five years after unveiling a plan to open the Trump on the Ocean catering hall at Jones Beach, the site is little more than a hole in the sand, and civic leaders say they are tired of waiting."

- tied the state government up in litigation

So much winning. Somehow many New Yorkers can't stand the man, or his former henchman Sorial. I do wonder why.

Elsewhere in his home state, golf course building again proved to be too much for Team Trump.

Ferry Point Golf

Not even drafting in Jack Nicklaus could win the day; New York State taxpayers are more than a little teed off at having spent some $97 million on this project. Various companies came and went over the decades, and finally Trump built a course (expect to pay about $200 for a round). Enjoy a day out at this former rubbish tip, where methane gas is released through pipes situated here and there. Pollution, delays, ignoring environmental protection seem to be the standard.

Elsewhere in the Tri State Area Trump's golf projects have seen trees felled which were expressly earmarked not to be felled; acre on acre of wetlands compromised, litigation drawn out, fines and more.

As ProPublica put it: "On May 29, 2009, Edward Russo, then Trump's environmental consultant, "self-reported" damage to 4.34 acres of wetlands, open waters and wetland transition areas. In doing so, the Trump Organization was seeking forgiveness under a DEP policy that allows as much as a 100 percent reduction in fines for offenders who voluntarily disclose violations "in a timely manner" and correct them promptly. Subsequent violations would not be self-reported in a timely manner — indeed, they wouldn't be self-reported at all…"

What a pity that environmental expert Bill Ritchie, whose premise to the Scottish reporters boiled down to 'it's fine to let Trump build on the SSSI site, we'll just monitor the environmental aspects' wasn't such an expert that he did any research into Trump and saw what the rest of us who knew him from New York knew would happen.

New Jersey (aka Noo Joysee)

<u>Atlantic City</u>

Some say gambling, organised crime and Donald J Trump ruined this seaside town. Hard to argue. He had several casinos; people backed them because of the Trump name ('go figure' as we say in New York). It all fell apart.

The New York Times said of the bellicose billionaire's behaviour there: "But even as his companies did poorly, Mr. Trump did well. He put up little of his own money, shifted personal debts to the casinos and collected millions of dollars in salary, bonuses and other payments. The burden of his failures fell on investors and others who had bet on his business acumen."

Winning it seems has little to do with moral fibre, heroics, doing what's right, and everything to do with covering your own arse, however large it is.

People hooked on gambling, a seaside town on its uppers. Small businesses hurt when Trump entities went bankrupt while the man and his family were insulated from bankruptcy themselves. Some people might think of this as an ethically-bankrupt sh*tstorm of a disaster. I guess Sorial thought this was leadership, success and winning. What does The Donald say?

"I do play with the bankruptcy laws — they're very good for me" --

http://www.thedailybeast.com/newsweek/2011/04/24/the-trump-backlash.html

Florida

<u>Mar-a-Lago</u>

Trump and his fondness for giant erections saw him embroiled in a multi-million-dollar lawsuit with the state government. Some would say that a good lawyer will ensure that you comply with local laws, don't aggravate potential customers, don't engage in frivolous litigation, and don't make a complete arse of yourself. Sorial's brand of winning comes from a different school of thought.

Trump's side represented: "Trump's lawsuit maintained that he couldn't bring his flag and pole into compliance with regulations because "A smaller flag and pole on Mar-A-Lago's property would be lost given its massive size, look silly instead of make a statement, and most importantly would fail to appropriately express the magnitude of Donald J. Trump's and the Club's members' patriotism." – it is a credit to Mr Sorial that he can be part of a team that can deliver such a statement with a straight face.

Who would want or need an 80-foot flagpole? What are they

compensating for? This isn't Mar-a-Lago; it's Menie – but if the scale of this thing seems pompous, pseud-patriotic and fugly, that's because it is

The other goings on at Mar-a-Lago could make you wonder whether Trump has any national security advisors or lawyers at all. In 2017 the House Oversight Committee launched an investigation into his alleged security breaches at the club.

The Independent reported: "After it was revealed that the President discussed North Korea's ballistic missile test over dinner with Japanese Prime Minister Shinzo Abe and other guests in what committee chairman Jason Chaffetz described as a "public space", the committee has asked the President's team to provide proof of his security protocols at his estate and how they were maintained."

George was somehow meant to be involved in ensuring compliance. Trump seemed more chummy than compliant when appointing members of his Mar-a-Lago club to what USA today called 'plum' jobs.

The publication reported: "A USA TODAY review finds that Trump has installed at least five people who have been members of his clubs to senior roles in his administration, ranging from Bernstein and Callista Gingrich, the nation's new ambassador to the Vatican, to Adolfo Marzol, a member of the Trump National Golf Club in suburban Washington, who serves as a senior adviser at the Department of Housing and Urban Development.

"Presidents often name campaign donors and close allies to administration posts, particularly prized diplomatic postings in cosmopolitan European capitals, such as Paris and London, and the tourist playgrounds of the West Indies.

"But never in modern history has a president awarded government posts to people who pay money to his own companies."

Mexico

Trump Ocean Resort Baja Mexico was meant to be a hotel/ condominium. It flopped.

When it was clear the ship was sinking with cost over runs and other issues, Trump removed his name from the development late in 2008.

Investors who had made down payments averaging over $200,000 per person claimed they believed Trump – whose name was on the project – was involved. He claimed he merely licensed his name and disavowed any financial or indeed moral responsibility. Donald Trump, Jr. and Ivanka plus the Trump Organization were defendants in a case that ensued in California. The suit was settled out of court for an undisclosed sum. As you do if you're a conquering hero of a winner with a great lawyer. As an aside, I'm no lawyer – but could licencing your name, especially if your forte is bankruptcies, not be a very very handy mechanism for money laundering? Just a thought.

This list of 'wins' could go on for several pages, but the picture should be clear by now. Trump's ties to Saudi Arabia have been deliberately left out of this little book; we will leave that to the authorities who are currently investigating. One thing to remember is that Congress wanted Trump to provide a report into the murder of journalist Jamal Khashoggi; he refused.

Adam Schiff, or 'Little Adam Schitt' as Drumpf called him is said by The Atlantic to have questions: "The president is not being honest with the country about the murder of Jamal Khashoggi," Schiff said "Is his personal financial interest driving U.S. policy in the Gulf? ... Are there financial entanglements with the Gulf? Are there financial inducements that the president has not to want to cross the Saudis?"

Bloomberg summed the unacceptable situation up: "Jamal Khashoggi's death has exposed the White House and two of its most powerful figures as naive, ill-informed and craven. What comes next?"

We'll see how Trump wins his way out of that.

IV Afterthoughts

Writing this story in this format is something I'd never predicted. For the past few years I've half-started books on Aberdeen Voice, Trump in Scotland and related subjects but until now have never had that burning need to collate these anecdotes into a reference volume / chronicle as fast as possible. The speed will no doubt show in the writing, but it's 30 March, and without fail, this book is being launched in early June, prior to the Trump book by Sorial and Bates. This is not negotiable; I have to finish this soon.

A reader will notice that themes appear under more than one heading. My hope is to have written the sort of book a reader can dip in and out of, depending on which subject they are interested in. This is why there are areas of overlap. For my own purposes, this book is a means to formalise all the research I've done to make a handy guide for future writing.

Satire is something Trump can't stand – yet uses brutal bullying with impunity. My satires have been crude, trying at times to be caustic (admittedly kind of amateurish), not kind. But satire remains one protected weapon against the powerful, particularly wielded well by people in Scotland.

Now to my more important last thought: Trump's verbal attacks on the media. If you've managed to get this far through my book, you'll have an idea how I feel about hate speech and where it takes the gullible, the weak, the bully, the manipulative, the violent, and how I feel about self-serving people masquerading as professional journalists. Trump wants his version of events to be the one that time remembers. He can hire writers married to his spokeswoman to pen lovely full colour, glossy hardbacks. I'll be writing on my way to and from work, putting this out as economically as I can. I feel that I can't allow the guy who shouts longest and loudest to have their glossy, hard-cover version of events drown out documentary evidence without at least putting up a fight backed up with evidence. This is why there are so many quotes and extracts. If people come to conclusions other than what I have – this is great, as long as it's based on the facts.

Aberdeen city and Shire are funny places. Aside from the efforts of small, online Aberdeen Voice, the local printed press, the Press and Journal and Evening Express, are the only newspapers. In my opinion these papers have historically put development over environment to put it mildly. Readers are often told that when oil runs out Aberdeen must have other reasons for people to live and work in the area; somehow these are always it seems at the expense of wildlife and land. These schemes seem to be run by the same cabal of businessmen. Things could be better.

Help make things better by dropping a postcard to the Forbes/Milnes/Munros at the Menie Estate. Boycott Trump locations and goods. Tell your elected rep, especially if you're in Aberdeenshire, what you think of the plans for Menie. Join Tripping Up Trump. Every act is an act of defiance; every absence of action is a declaration you are happy with things the way they are and/or are not interested.

Thank you for reading my book.

PS – should anyone in Trumpton wants to sue me, form an orderly cue. Remember everything in this book is my own fact-based firmly-held belief, that everything here is 100% in the public interest, and that I – for the foreseeable future – still have an EU human right of freedom of expression. Not that any tyrants fond of freedom of expression on US campuses would dare to challenge mine. So, sue me. You can have my debt, my collection of beer bottles, and my record collection. If you win.

http://www.thedailybeast.com/newsweek/2011/04/24/the-trump-backlash.html

Suzanne G Kelly

30 May 2019

APPENDIX

I. Email 3 March 2013 from Aberdeenshire planner to S Kelly

I acknowledge that the developer at the Menie Estate has, on a number of occasions, applied for planning permission which has been granted and subsequently the works that have been carried out are not in accordance with the approved plans. In all these instances the Planning Service has sought to address this situation by the submission of retrospective applications. Such applications are, unfortunately, relatively common where it has been identified that works have been undertaken in breach of planning control. Normal practice in such situations to remedy the breach is through the grant of planning permission with any appropriate conditions.

Many retrospective applications are submitted following an investigation in relation to a complaint, or to reduce the likelihood of the Local Authority commencing enforcement action. In the case of this development I can assure you that it has been closely monitored. The Planning Service has followed up on all allegations of breaches of planning control including non-compliance with conditions or development which has been undertaken in breach of permission which has been granted. As previously indicated this may result in a retrospective

application being submitted to regularise the works undertaken, or a subsequent application to allow the development to be undertaken without complying with a specific condition(s).

You have highlighted a number of other possible contraventions of planning permission at the Menie Estate and I will comment on these in turn:-

1. Construction of bunds by Munro Home (Leyton Cottage)

Bunds were detailed on the drawings for the access road / car park planning permission which was approved. The bunds that have been formed on site deviated from these and are the subject of a live retrospective planning application which is being considered by the Planning Service.

2. Construction of bunds by Milne Home (Hermit's Point)

This Service is aware that bunds were erected at this point. However these have now been removed.

3. Planting trees on bunds at above locations

Planting of trees is not considered to be development. Therefore no planning permission is required.

4. Planting of Sycamore trees on bunds near Milne home

As outlined above the planting of trees is not considered to be development. Therefore, no planning permission is required. As such the Planning Service cannot control the type of tree which is planted. [very coy indeed; the issue was planting on the ridiculously high bunds

5. Planting trees (possibly 100+) by Milne home

As above planting of trees is not development therefore, no planning permission is required. As no planning permission is required, the Planning Service has no remit to consider whether or not any environmental change will take place or any effect on the blockage of light.

6. Allowing construction vehicles to cause deterioration of Leyton Road, improper renovation/temporary resurfacing of

same

A complaint was previously investigated on this issue. Following enquiries it was established that the roads referred to were private estate roads over which there is a public access to properties. There had been increased construction traffic etc but also a combination of severe weather which had also taken its toll.

The developer confirmed that remedial works would be undertaken to the roads particularly where property owners require continual access to improve the condition of the roads. In essence this was a private civil matter. The conclusion of this matter was that the breach was resolved and the road damage reinstated and to a better level than previously.

7. Replacement of a traditional outbuilding near Leyton Road with a corrugated metal structure

This matter was also investigated and the works undertaken were considered to be repairs to an existing building with the subsequent use being covered by the overarching permission that was granted for the use of the land as a golf course. [not everyone would agree]

8. Construction of parking lot

The car park was constructed other than in accordance with the original approval. However retrospective planning permission has been sought. [and Trump seems to get all of his after-the-fact plans approved: why?]

9. Entrance sign – larger than originally agreed

Signage was erected other than in accordance with the Advertisement Consent approved. An application for retrospective Advertisement Consent was submitted and has been approved.

10. Temporary clubhouse – was it approved in advance?

The temporary clubhouse was erected other than in accordance with the original approval. However retrospective planning permission has been sought and approved. [do other than you have permission for first, get permission second; Aberdeenshire will ok it. If you are Trump]

11. Vegetation stripped away from area north of Leyton cottage

As part of planning permission environmental monitoring by a third party was undertaken throughout the construction of the golf course. The Ecological Clerk of Works has highlighted no issues. Copies of these reports are available on line via the following link.

http://www.aberdeenshire.gov.uk/planning/apps/detail.asp?ref_no=APP/2006/4605

12. Use of culverts instead of bridges on course

Again the environmental monitoring by the Ecological Clerk of Works has highlighted no issues in this regard. [Is the Ecological Clerk of Works position monitored independently? Does Trump fund this post? No clear answers were ever given]

Finally I note that you have requested a meeting with the Planning Service. However I do not consider that this would be necessary given that the issues you have raised are in the majority of cases historic and the breaches of planning resolved through the submission and approval of applications or indeed the removal of unauthorised works.

I can assure you that Aberdeenshire Council and the Planning Service

monitor this site [Sorry, I don't feel remotely assured] and will continue to do so to ensure that works are carried out in accordance with the permissions granted [so: it's monitored but they did some 11 things that exceeded permission despite the monitoring] and to take necessary action where breaches occur [Sure. Like issuing permission after the fact]. The Service enforces planning and building regulations and access legislation in an equal and fair manner throughout the authority and all situations are dealt with in a consistent manner. [HA HA HA]

II. Scottish Enterprise Grampian to S Kelly, on Sorial using its logo, video of head

"Neither SE, nor Ms Craw, has endorsed the Trump planning application [well if Perry didn't endorse and push it, what do they call what he did?] SE Grampian is supportive of the proposals but they have no role or remit in terms of the planning decision [yet Perry sent 'personal' notes to support it to various parties].

"Ms Craw gave an interview to STV in relation to a documentary on the Trump International plans for a golf leisure development on 26 June 2006. Ms Craw was not made aware that the clip would be used as part of the Trump presentation at the public meeting. [Experienced lawyer Sorial somehow got hold of the video and decided to show it in public without any attempt at getting clearance from SE or Craw?]

"SE has not endorsed the planning application. [they're repeating themselves] Any endorsement by Scottish Enterprise would not bind the Scottish Government. [but a government quango with a massive budget is not without influence]

"Donald Trump's organisation has not received any funding from SE Grampian. A Preliminary Feasibility study along with a promotional DVD in relation to the Menie Estate Golf Resort was commissioned by SE Grampian in line with support for inward investment activity. The cost of this was £30,285 [as other golf courses went bust, a billionaire got £30K out of the taxpayer].

"SE Grampian PR support [I'm still working out how you can provide PR support for something you are not endorsing] around the project announcement was given to the Trump Organisation in keeping with support offered to potential inward investors. Please note there is no monetary value placed on staff time spent on projects. [maybe there should be for transparency and accounting purposes]"

III. Aberdeen Voice Article Milne Petition: What the Committee Didn't Let You See

The full article can be found here https://aberdeenvoice.com/2013/09/milne-petition-committee-didnt-let-see/

Menie Police FOI Update: Little Info, No Confidence

Aberdeenshire, Featured, Opinion

You might think that if someone came onto your land, damaged goods and removed property – and you had a video which could hold vital evidence, the police would want to look at the tape. You would be wrong. If you were called David Milne and living on the Menie Estate. On behalf of David Milne, Suzanne Kelly tried to find out why there was no follow up and why no one would so much as touch the videotape.

After waiting several months for information requests and a Scottish Information Commissioner review, all we know is the information is too sensitive and too secret to reveal.

Put yourself in David Milne's place. You're living in a beautiful, protected environment; a sparsely populated coastal area north of Aberdeen. Then, Donald Trump arrives, with plans for a massive development (two golf courses, hundreds of homes, a clubhouse and hotel) and includes the homes and property of you and your neighbours in his development plan.

The national and local governments welcome Trump, and his promises, with open arms.

Next, the police create a special policy for policing the area; they claim to want to deter and detect crime at Menie. Security Guards then appear, randomly demanding identification from fellow residents. They spy on properties from their vans, and signs warning of CCTV recording go up.

Gates are erected and locked shut. One of your main access roads, formerly a well maintained dirt road is turned into an impassable rutted mess, undoubtedly due in part to construction vehicles. Months go by before it is repaired.

Next, Trump claims in the press that his property is being vandalised (which makes you wonder just why his security guards are watching the residents while vandals caused damage).

Police start to visit your neighbours, the Forbes Family, and eventually arrest Michael Forbes for taking property markers from land he is using and believes to be his – he is charged, but the case is later dropped.

Journalists you've met and have talked with are arrested and charged with 'breach of the peace'. Their offence seems to have been asking the site manager when the residents can expect their water back on – it had been off for 7 days.

Photographer Alicia Bruce is dissuaded from making a police complaint although a violent-tempered Trump groundskeeper has threatened her and threatened to smash her camera.

In October 2010 someone has gone onto your property, caused damage, and removed property; someone who just might be linked to the Trump development – which soon erects a cheap fence and sends you the bill for it. You have a video which shows some, or part of, the potentially criminal activity.

The full article can be found here: https://aberdeenvoice.com/2013/12/menie-police-foi-update-little-info-confidence/

This book is a product of MilHouse Publishing who can be contacted via their website at www.milhousepublishing.com, which is also where you can see some of the other products they have available.

Some of these are shown on the next few pages:-

Old Susannah's Handbook of Modern manners

Available on Amazons Kindle store

Manners and courtesy have taken a bruising of late. Old Susannah,
columnist, interviewer and investigative writer for Aberdeen Voice,
gets to grips with modern manners with a humorous handbook.

Postcards from Freedonia

Available on Amazons kindle Store

How did the USA get into the messes its in? These illustrated letters from John Murray, my art professor and friend paint a picture of the roots of our many problems. If you want to understand the present and predict the future, know the past

Postcards from Freedonia

Exxon Mobil, Shell and BP feeding on the remains of Iraq

Selected Letters & Mail Art of Professor John Murray
Artist, Professor, Marx Brothers Fan, Beer Drinker, Friend

A folio to dip in and out of for those living in interesting times

Collated by Suzanne Kelly

"Blinded by the Bling??"

ISBN 978-0-9559269-0-7

"Blinded by the Bling??" is a short factual book about the destruction of a Site of Special Scientific Interest in order to build a housing development and golf course in the North East of Scotland. This book takes the reader from the first approaches of the developer through the early stages of the planning process up to the point at which a Public Local Inquiry was about to start in the summer of 2008.

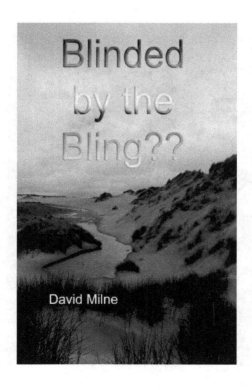

"It's Only Sand"

ISBN 978-0-9559269-1-4

"It's Only Sand" is a fictional novel set in an imaginary
country not far from here where a foreign multi billionaire
developer arrives with the intention of building 'the best
resort in the world' assuming that his 'usual methods' will
work just as well as anywhere else; but he hasn't bargained
on the locals and their determined attitude. So who wins out
in the end? Is it the international developer or the easy going,
relaxed locals?